Praise for *The Smart Nonprofit*

"AI is a complicated but necessary technology. It can be used to make people and nonprofits experience better, but if used without ethical implementation, it can destroy lives and harm the very people it is designed to help. This book works to describe this delicate balance. *The Smart Nonprofit* helps nonprofits think about how to use this technology with intention while explaining how to avoid the pitfalls that are possible. A human-centered focus is how all technology should be deployed."

Shireen Mitchell,
founder, Digital Sisters/as and Stop Online Violence Against Women

"In *The Smart Nonprofit*, Beth Kanter and Allison Fine bring attention to a looming transformation that is underappreciated in the social sector. Kanter and Fine have put their finger on the fundamental tension between the calling of our sector and the know-how to leverage AI and other smart technologies for good. Read this book. It's about the future and fate of the social sector writ large."

Mari Kuraishi,
president, Jesse Ball DuPont Fund

"We always joke about machines taking over our jobs. The truth is more interesting and complicated than that, as Beth Kanter and Allison Fine explore in this vital and timely book. With our sector relying more and more on technology and data, it is critical all of us are informed of the many ways smart tech could enable us to be more efficient at helping people, or unintentionally hurting them, especially those from marginalized communities. This is a thought-provoking and necessary book."

Vu Le,
NonprofitAF blog

"As decision-making becomes increasingly automated, it is critical that we are intentional about designing and using smart tech in the way that benefits our society and the planet. *The Smart Nonprofit: Staying Human Centered in an Automated World* is an exceptional read for nonprofit leaders who are looking to understand challenges and opportunities of smart tech, including how to design and use technologies such as artificial intelligence and machine learning in a responsible, humane, and impactful way."

Leila Toplic,
head of Emerging Technologies Initiative
NetHope

"The adaptation and understanding of smart tech enables social sector leaders to make quantum leaps forward in meeting their missions and fostering cultures of innovation and abundance. But just knowing that isn't enough. Kanter and Fine have given us the road map: practical, actionable advice for the tech-savvy and non-techies alike, and organizations large and small will benefit."

Asha Curran,
CEO, Giving Tuesday

"Beth Kanter and Allison Fine's new book provides a refreshingly nuanced view on the use of data and AI in the nonprofit sector. The timely question the authors seek to answer is not whether nonprofits need to develop good data management practices and a pervasive data use culture but how to transform their operations and strive for impact. Kanter and Fine's smart nonprofit is one that realizes the opportunities that data offers and knows how to mitigate the risks."

Claudia Juech,
vice president, data and society,
Patrick J. McGovern Foundation

"Finally, a book that cuts through the hype about AI and gives commonsense guidance to nonprofit leaders on how they can get smarter in how they use tech to power their organizations."

Micah Sifry,
cofounder, Civic Hall

"Beth Kanter and Allison Fine have given a powerful road map for nonprofit leaders on how to navigate the adoption of artificial intelligence and other smart technologies. With this book in hand, nonprofits will be able to turn the page on the era of frantic busyness to one in which they have time to think and plan and even dream."

Charlene Li,
New York Times best-selling author of
The Disruption Mindset and *Founder of Altimeter*

"An absolutely vital read for all nonprofit executives. AI and other smart technologies are here to stay, and understanding how they can impact your employees, donors, and grantees will be vital for your future success. Allison Fine and Beth Kanter break down all you need to know in a format that is digestible and actionable."

Susan McPherson,
CEO, McPherson Strategies and author of
The Lost Art of Connecting

"The inevitable introduction of more automation needn't dehumanize your nonprofit. As Kanter and Fine show us, knowing how to incorporate technology into our processes appropriately can free us up to do the things that only people can do and in ways that enhance the deeper connections between us."

Douglas Rushkoff,
author of *Team Human*,
Present Shock, and *Program or Be Programed*

"Since I see technology itself as amoral, I believe its impact (positive or negative) is a function of the ethics, values, and beliefs of those applying it. Using real-world examples, Kanter and Fine explore the promise and pitfalls of how nonprofits are using advanced digital technology, including artificial intelligence, machine learning, natural language processes, and bots."

Mario Morino,
Chair and CEO, Morino Institute

"Beth Kanter and Allison Fine have written the definitive guide for nonprofit leaders on how to navigate the adoption of artificial intelligence and other smart technologies. With this book in hand, nonprofits will be able to raise money, deliver effective programs, and run their back offices efficiently while staying human-centered."

Jeremiah Owyang,
tech analyst, founding partner of Kaleido Insights

"Automation can be a crucial resource for managers and employees who are adapting to a changing workplace—but only if we anticipate and address its risks to equity, inclusion and effectiveness. This book will help leaders make the most of smart tech's potential: It's essential reading for anyone who works in a mission-driven organization, or for those who want to understand the way automation will transform the non-profit sector."

Alexandra Samuel,
PhD and coauthor of *Remote,*
Inc.: How to Thrive at Work. . .Wherever You Are

"Beth and Allison completely redefined the nonprofit technology game with their must-read book *The Networked Nonprofit*. And with their newest book, they do it again. *The Smart Nonprofit* is the perfect field guide for nonprofits who struggle to tackle the perils of tech automation, standardization, and the ethical quandaries that come with it. Beth and Allison answer, with case studies and rich examples, how we can best adopt this smart technology intentionally and carefully—while avoiding embedded bias and maintaining ethical standards. I highly recommend this book to any nonprofit or social change agent looking to answer the questions of how to leverage automation and technology to save time and better accomplish their missions but who want to remain human-centered as well."

Julia Campbell,
speaker, author, nonprofit consultant

"At a cultural moment for trying to understand AI, here's a great primer for nonprofit leaders, especially to think about how smart tech can be harnessed in human ways."

Peter Simms,
author and founder and CEO of Black Sheep (BLK SHP)

"Artificial intelligence and other smart technologies are a critical part of our everyday lives. AI is becoming instrumental to all industries and sectors, including the nonprofit space. In this book, Beth and Allison illuminate the potential of what smart tech could do—and indeed, is already doing—for social and environmental good. *The Smart Nonprofit* provides practical, actionable (and timely) advice for all nonprofit leaders—I couldn't recommend it enough."

Carlos Miranda,
cofounder and chairman, Lightful

"The issues raised by Beth Kanter and Allison Fine in their new book should be at the top of any nonprofit leader's list of priorities. Online platforms such as GlobalGiving are engaged in active debate about them already, but as our technological tools continue to advance and their applications become more ubiquitous, all nonprofits should consider themselves digital organizations. We could all use additional guidance on these tricky questions."

Alix Guerrier,
CEO, DonorsChoose

"*The Smart Nonprofit* is a must-read for the 21st-century organization, addressing both the ethical and practical challenges of artificial intelligence. Beth Kanter and Allison Fine—veterans in providing vital tools to nonprofit leaders—have done it again, breaking down the complicated world of smart tech into bite-sized, actionable strategies that will become the gold standard in the sector."

Kathleen Kelly Janus,
author of *Social Startup Success: How the Best Nonprofits Launch, Scale and Make a Difference*

"*The Smart Nonprofit* could not be timelier for anyone involved in social change efforts. This book is filled with practical examples of how smart tech is already being deployed to tackle social challenges and where we can go from here. This is a terrific, timely book that comes at a critical moment for us as a sector and as a society."

Vinay Nair,
CEO and cofounder, Lightful

"Beth Kanter and Allison Fine provide a practical guide for the future in *The Smart Nonprofit: Staying Human-Centered in an Automated World*. This book is a valuable resource for nonprofit organizational leaders to understand the challenges and opportunities of smart tech and how they can harness this potential to advance their missions. *The Smart Nonprofit* is filled with examples and case studies that help paint a picture of the possibilities with AI and provides inspiration for anyone considering how they may effectively make use of smart tech for their organization."

Jason Shim,
coauthor of *Bitcoin and the Future of Fundraising*

"In *The Smart Nonprofit*, Beth Kanter and Allison Fine demystify the moment we are in by helping nonprofit leaders understand how to use smart technology to center people and their values, reduce bias, and unlock time so that staff can focus on imagining new solutions and enhancing the overall experience people have with their organizations. Whether you are concerned about the limitations and the unintentional harmful consequences of the technology or are looking for a practical guide to apply smart tech, you won't regret reading this book."

Farra Trompeter,
codirector, member-owner, Big Duck

THE SMART NON- PROFIT

THE SMART NON- PROFIT

Staying Human-Centered in an Automated World

BETH KANTER | ALLISON FINE

WILEY

Published by John Wiley & Sons, Inc., Hoboken, New Jersey.
Published simultaneously in Canada.

For general information on our other products and services or for technical support, please contact our Customer Care Department within the United States at (800) 762-2974, outside the United States at (317) 572-3993, or fax (317) 572-4002.

Wiley also publishes its books in a variety of electronic formats. Some content that appears in print may not be available in electronic formats. For more information about Wiley products, visit our web site at www.wiley.com.

Library of Congress Cataloging-in-Publication Data

Names: Kanter, Beth, 1957- author. | Fine, Allison H., 1964- author.
Title: The smart nonprofit : staying human-centered in an automated world / Beth Kanter and Allison Fine.
Description: Hoboken, New Jersey : Wiley, [2022] | Includes bibliographical references and index.
Identifiers: LCCN 2021052478 (print) | LCCN 2021052479 (ebook) | ISBN 9781119818120 (cloth) | ISBN 9781119818144 (adobe pdf) | ISBN 9781119818137 (epub)
Subjects: LCSH: Nonprofit organizations. | Organizational change.
Classification: LCC HD2769.15 .K37 2022 (print) | LCC HD2769.15 (ebook) | DDC 658/.048—dc23/eng/20211028
LC record available at https://lccn.loc.gov/2021052478
LC ebook record available at https://lccn.loc.gov/2021052479

Cover image(s): © Getty Images | Tuomas A. Lehtinen
Cover design: Paul McCarthy
SKY10030951_011722

We dedicate this book to the millions of staff members, board members, and volunteers of nonprofits who do the hard work every day and with the smart use of smart tech can now work smarter. Thank you for making the world safer, smarter, happier, healthier, and fairer.

CONTENTS

PREFACE

For the last four years, we have been tracking the use of digital technologies like artificial intelligence, what we call "smart tech" in this book, for social good. Smart tech is very quickly becoming embedded in nonprofit operations. It is helping them automate tasks such as screening clients for services, filling out expense reports, and identifying prospective donors. Sometimes organizations are intentionally choosing to add smart tech to their efforts, but more often we are finding that smart tech is sneaking into organizations without organizations realizing it.

This moment feels familiar. We have been writing about the wide scale adoption of social media since the early 2000s. We know the patterns of technology adoption: there are small commercial vendors with funny names overhyping the benefits and underplaying the risks, there are a few early adopters finding clever ways to use the technology, and there is the enormous ecosystem of nonprofits and foundations who are resistant to change and technology.

We believed smart tech was part of the ongoing march of technology that makes organizations go faster and become more efficient until we had a talk with our friend Steve MacLaughlin, vice president of product management at Blackbaud. He told us during a podcast interview in October 2020 that the benefit of using smart tech isn't about increasing speed and scale; it's about time.

Smart tech is going to take over time-consuming rote tasks that are taking hours to do right now, freeing up enormous amounts of staff time. Steve calls this the "AI dividend." We call it the "dividend of time" in this book. Whatever you call it, the idea is profound and potentially revolutionary.

The choices organizations make about how to use their dividend of time is the key to the next stage in organizational life. We can choose to continue our frantic pace of work, responding to crises and flooding inboxes with email solicitations. Or we can choose to use this new time to reduce staff burnout, get to know clients on a deeper, human level, and focus on solving problems like homelessness in addition to serving homeless people. And as far-fetched as it may seem, we believe nonprofits can use this time to become the leaders in the ethical and responsible use of smart tech, the most powerful technology everyday people and organizations have ever used. Taken altogether, this is the essence of being a smart nonprofit.

We have a once-in-a-generation opportunity to remake work but only for those people and organizations that are thoughtful and knowledgeable about the use of smart tech. It also raises existential questions such as: When should machines do the work people do now? How can we be actively anti-biased using smart tech? What can we do differently or better with our new time? We hope this book gives you and your colleagues a solid foundation for understanding and answering these kinds of questions.

We hope the increased dividend of time will be spent doing the things that only people can do: building strong relationships, dreaming up new solutions, creating and strengthening communities. We want to turn the page on our era of frantic busyness and scarcity to one in which smart nonprofits have the time to think and plan and even dream.

ACKNOWLEDGMENTS

All books are difficult to write. Add a pandemic on top of it, and a special kind of endurance is required. We are extremely grateful to our colleagues and friends and family who supported us during the writing of this book.

You can't write a book during a global pandemic without the very patient support of your family. Allison would like to thank all of her Freiman boys for their patience and encouragement during the very long sheltering in place. Beth would like to thank her husband, Walter, and her children, Harry and Sara, who gave her the time and space to write.

A special thanks to Brian Neill, Deborah Schindlar, Kelly Talbot, and the rest of the team at Wiley. We are very grateful for your enthusiasm for this book and our long partnership with the company. Onward!

We'd also like to thank our book assistant, Kait Heacock, for her terrific work,

This book would not have been possible without the early investment in our work on smart tech and philanthropy by Victoria Vrana and Parastou Youssefi at the Bill & Melinda Gates Foundation. They and their team are thoughtful, prescient innovators and advocates for the democratization of philanthropy.

We are very grateful for the time and input of experts working at the intersection of technology and social good. They are doing the hard work everyday of healing the world. In particular, we are thankful to: Alexandra Goodwin, Allen Gunn, Anna Bethke, Anurag Banerjee, Brigitte Hoyer Gosselink, Cinthia

Schuman, Chris Tuttle, Christopher Noessel, Darrell Malone, David A Colarusso, France Q. Hoang, Heejae Lim, Iain De Jong, Jake Garcia, Jake Maguire, Jill Finlayson, John Mayer, Julie Cordua, Kevin Bromer, Leah Post, Leila Toplic, Mohammad Radiyat, Nancy Smyth, Nick Bailey, Nick Hamlin, Ravindar Gujral, Rhodri Davies, Rita Ko, Shalini Kantayya, Steve MacLaughlin, Sue Citro, and Woodrow Rosenbaum.

We want to give a special thanks to friends and colleagues who read parts of this book, answered questions, and gave us advice (when we asked for it and when we didn't!). In particular, we'd like to thank: Tamara Gropper, Mark Polisar, Lucy Bernholz, Johanna Morariu, Lisa Belkin, and Amy Sample Ward for their input and advice.

PART I

UNDERSTANDING AND USING ARTIFICIAL INTELLIGENCE

CHAPTER 1

Becoming a Smart Nonprofit

INTRODUCTION

Leah Post has a keen sense of other people's pain. As a program manager at a Seattle social service nonprofit, she uses her gifts to help people who are homeless, or at high risk of homelessness, enter the local support system. An integral part of the intake process is a required assessment tool with the tongue-twisting name VI-SPDAT.

Every day, Leah asked her clients questions from the VI-SPDAT and inputted their answers into the computer. And every day the results didn't match the picture of despair she saw in front of her, the results that should have made her clients top priorities for receiving emergency housing.

Leah knew the basic statistics for the homeless population in King County, home to Seattle. Black people are 6% of the general population but over a third of the homeless population. For Native Americans or Alaska Natives that ratio is 1 to 10. Most of Leah's clients were Black, and yet time and again white applicants scored higher on the VI-SPDAT, meaning they would receive services first. Leah knew in her gut that something was wrong, and yet automated systems are supposed to be impartial, aren't they?

With over a decade of experience as a social worker, Leah knows that asking people who are scared, in pain, may have mental illness, and are at your mercy to self-report their personal struggles is not likely to yield accurate results. Similarly, victims of domestic violence were unlikely to self-report an abusive relationship. But that's not how the VI-SPDAT worked. For instance, one of the questions was: "Has your drinking or drug use led you to being kicked out of an apartment or program where you were staying in the past?" Single, adult Black Indigenous People of Color (BIPOC) were 62% less likely than white applicants to answer yes.[1] In general, denial of drinking and drug use is the smarter and safer answer for people of color when applying for public benefits. Except when taking the VI-SPDAT. This assessment is intended to measure vulnerability, which means the higher the score, the more urgently a client needs housing. But, Leah says, VI-SPDAT "just doesn't allow the space for any interpretation of answers."[2]

Leah was not the only person noticing skewed results. Dozens of social workers joined her in signing a petition in Seattle asking for a review of the process. Other social workers around the country also raised concerns. Finally, researchers at C4 Innovations dug into the data from King County, as well as counties in Oregon, Virginia, and Washington, and found that BIPOC "were 32% less likely than their White counterparts to receive a high prioritization score, despite their overrepresentation in the homeless population."

There were red flags about the VI-SPDAT from the beginning. It was evidence-informed, not evidence-based, meaning it was built on information and experiences from past efforts but neither rigorously designed nor tested. It was intended for quick triage but was most often used as an overall assessment tool by social service agencies. No training was required to use it. Oh, and it was free.[3]

Why was King County, or any county, using a tool with so many red flags? Some of the answer is found in its development history.

The Department of Housing and Urban Development (HUD) provides funding for homelessness to local communities through Continuums of Care (CoCs) consortia of local agencies. This system was created in the 1990s to provide multiple access points for people who are homeless, or at risk of homelessness, through, say, food banks, homeless shelters, or mental health clinics.

In 2009, HUD began to require CoCs to use a standardized assessment tool to prioritize the most vulnerable people. This was an important switch from the traditional "first come, first serve" model. The wait for emergency housing can be years long, and having an opportunity to get to the top of the list is a very big deal for clients. The choice of which tool to use was left up to each CoC.

Years earlier, Community Solutions, a New York nonprofit specializing in using data to reduce homelessness, created the Vulnerability Index (VI) based on peer-reviewed research. The goal of the VI was to lower barriers for people with physical or mental health vulnerabilities that might prevent them from seeking services. Soon afterward, OrgCode Consulting, Inc., created the Service Prioritization Decision Assistance Tool (SPDAT). Finally, in 2013, OrgCode released a combination of these tools, the VI-SPDAT.

The president of OrgCode, Iain De Jong, told us that time was of the essence in launching VI-SPDAT, which precluded more robust testing and training materials.[4] By 2015 more than one thousand communities across the United States, Canada, and Australia were using the VI-SPDAT.

The VI-SPDAT was initially released as a downloadable document with a manual scoring index because contrary to its name, OrgCode isn't a tech company. Two years after its release, multiple software companies serving homeless agencies asked to incorporate the VI-SPDAT into their products, and OrgCode consented.

Incorporating the VI-SPDAT into software programs automated it, which meant that instead of scoring the assessment by hand, administrators were now restricted to inputting data into screens and leaving the rest up to the computer. VI-SPDAT became a smart tech tool. The power of decision-making shifted from people to computers. This gave the VI-SPDAT a patina of infallibility and impartiality. Jake Maguire of Community Solutions said, "There are people who have divorced the scoring tool from the basic infrastructure required for meaningful community problem solving. It is complex. What we need to do is to equip people with the skills and permissions that give them informed flexibility. Don't automatically surrender your better judgment and clinical judgment. We can't put our brains on autopilot when we use these tools."[5] As a result, thousands of BIPOC people didn't get the priority spot they deserved or access they needed to vital services.

You may be waiting for some bad guy to emerge in this story: a company gathering data to sell to pharmaceutical companies or a government agency intentionally blocking access to services. There will be stories like that later in this book, but this isn't one of them.

All the actors here had good intentions. HUD wanted to ease access into the homeless system by using multiple access points and placing local organizations in charge of the assessment. OrgCode was trying to create a standard tool for social workers and disseminate it easily, freely, and quickly. Leah and her colleagues were dedicated to helping the most vulnerable people in their communities receive appropriate services quickly. And, of course, clients who were walking in off the street just wanted to be safe at least for one night.

And yet, the VI-SPDAT was so fundamentally flawed that OrgCode announced in 2021 that it would no longer recommend or support it.

UNDERSTANDING SMART TECH

We use "smart tech" as an umbrella term for advanced digital technologies that make decisions *for* people, *instead* of people. It includes artificial intelligence (AI) and its subsets and cousins such as machine learning, natural language processing, smart forms, chatbots, robots, and drones. We want to be expansive in our use and understanding of the term, for instance, by including automation technologies like the one that powered the VI-SPDAT, in order to focus on the essence of the shift in power from people to machines. We substitute the word "bot" for smart tech in many sentences in this book because, well, it's fun to say.

Smart tech is not the same as digitizing a process. For instance, direct depositing a paycheck replaces printing a check and mailing it or handing it to an employee who has to endorse it and physically deposit it in the bank. Direct deposit is efficient, but it's not automation. Automation takes the power of decision-making and turns it over to machines. Automation turns a regular car into a smart car, and an active, decision-making driver into a passenger.

Netflix is powered by smart tech. They use our individual and collective viewing to make suggestions of what you may want to watch next. The more we all watch, the more accurate are Netflix's predictions. However, there is one enormous catch: the algorithms assume we want to continue watching the kinds of shows and movies we have in the past, that our future behavior will mimic past behavior. However, this isn't actually the way most people operate. We like to explore new things, bump into new people, and allow serendipity to take its course. This difference between the way machines think and the way people behave is a theme we will explore many times throughout this book.

Smart tech has some similarities with social media but more importantly, a few fundamental differences. Both are powered by digital technology, computer code, and enormous amounts of data. They also use the data and algorithms to predict future behavior. For instance, Facebook shows you ads based on what you have liked and shared previously. The more accurate Facebook's predictions, the more likely you are to click on an ad, which is how they make their money. However, we can see how Facebook operates or at least the results of Facebook's calculations. Even if Facebook doesn't want to put much work into controlling hate speech on its platform, we can see it unfolding on the platform. And if you can find the button to click to show you the most recent feeds, you can see which posts you've missed because Facebook decided to show you something else.

While social media is visible, smart tech is invisible like air. It doesn't care if you're rich or poor, at home in your kitchen, in the park, or at the office; it is everywhere around us working all the time. It is quickly becoming embedded in organizational life and making critical decisions such as who gets services, when and how, and how staff are performing their jobs. Perhaps the biggest difference between social media and smart tech is that the former creates an enormous amount of work while the latter, if used well, can create an enormous amount of time. And that time can be used to reduce burnout of staff; increase time spent with clients, volunteers, and donors; and imagine new ways to solve difficult problems.

Smart tech is best at doing rote tasks such as filling out intake forms and answering the same questions from people (for example, "Is my contribution tax-deductible?") over and over. However, the technology is quickly moving beyond paperwork and embedding itself into the heart of nonprofit work. This is profoundly changing what we do, why we do it, and how successful we are in meeting our missions.

Nonprofits are beginning to use smart tech to:

- Screen resumes based on criteria organizations set but without those organizations likely seeing the people who were screened out.

- Determine eligibility for a host of social services such as SNAP food assistance, housing, and childcare.

- Identify prospective donors from your fundraising data or from the web.

- Customize stories for and communications to donors based on their past behavior.

- Stock food pantry shelves.

- Deliver medicine and food to hard-to-reach places.

- Direct refugees to available beds.

This isn't science fiction; it is real life, right now.

Automating systems isn't a technological evolution; it is a revolutionary shift in power and autonomy. Those who understand the new technology and how to use it will have more power. Those who are reporting to tech systems and are at the mercy of them are at the risk of losing their ability to determine their own futures.

Smart nonprofits understand the technology—what it can and cannot do, how to use it well, and how to avoid unintentional harmful consequences.

Becoming a Smart Nonprofit

Smart nonprofits use a disciplined approach to adopting smart tech carefully and strategically while always maintaining the highest ethical standards and responsible use. Smart nonprofits are:

Human-centered: A human-centered approach means finding the sweet spot between people and smart tech, while ensuring that people are always in charge of the technology. Smart nonprofits ensure that the use of smart tech always aligns with their values.

Prepared: Organizations need to take intentional preparation steps. They must actively reduce bias embedded in smart tech code and systems. They also thoroughly correct and label data to be incorporated into a smart tech system. And lastly, they must have a formal process to select systems, vendors, and consultants that align with their organization's values.

Knowledgeable and reflective: Learning about what smart tech is and does is an ongoing process in the boardroom, the C-suite, and for nonprofit staffs. Once automated systems are in place, organizations need to be vigilant about whether they are performing as hoped or unintended consequences have arisen, and how clients and end users feel about the systems. We have embedded reflection questions throughout this book to help create the habit of asking important questions over time.

Working this way with smart tech creates a gift of new time.

Staff people spend about 30% of their time on administrative tasks. Smart tech is going to automate many of these tasks, thereby freeing up staff to do other things. This newly found time creates a choice for organizations. This new time could be used to do more of the same kinds of tasks that value efficiency over effectiveness and the number of people served over the number of problems solved. Or they can use this precious gift to become something new and better. We hope organizational leaders will choose the latter. We call this return on investment for the use of smart tech the *dividend of time*.[6]

Integrating smart tech into organizational functions could create an enormous return on investment that will allow for:

More time with clients: Instead of spending time checking off lists and filling out forms, case workers will spend more time with clients to understand the origins of their problems, the obstacles that get in the way of their success, and providing real-time support when life gets really hard.

Crisis prevention and reduction: Smart tech can help identify people at risk of becoming homeless before crises overwhelm them. For instance, the city of London, Ontario, uses a new smart tech system to track people at risk of becoming chronically homeless (with their permission) to prioritize services for them *before* a crisis.[7] Smart tech will help forecast environmental disasters earlier and help with rescue operations. Resources will be directed to victims faster.

Deeper and more meaningful relationships with donors: Transactional fundraising, treating every donor like an ATM machine, has become the norm for too many organizations. Smart tech frees staff from updating donor bases and researching prospects to spending time getting to know donors in meaningful ways: learning more about their interests and the reasons your cause is important to them and turning these donors into ambassadors to recruit and nurture donors within their personal networks.

Reduced astroturfing: Advocacy organizations too often substitute marketing efforts for real grassroots organizing. For instance, the use of online petitions that is actually used to capture email addresses for future communications. Instead of "astroturfing" support for climate change, advocates could use the dividend of time to engage with supporters and get to know them, educate them on the issue, and teach them how to become advocates and create their own group of supporters.

More time to think: People and organizations are so busy doing the work, and the work to support the work, that there is very little time for reflection on how the work is done and how to improve it. Imagine having time to consider other ways to do intake with clients rather than furiously responding to a barrage of inquiries every day? Imagine having time to talk to supporters about what kind of support they would need to gather their friends and help them become ambassadors? Imagine having time to just think.

A REAL-WORLD SMART NONPROFIT

TalkingPoints is a great example of a smart nonprofit.

Heejae Lim, founder of TalkingPoints, didn't need to do any research about the difficulty immigrant parents have navigating school systems; she lived it as the child of immigrants. Her family moved from Korea to London when she was eight.

Heejae had an advantage that many of her immigrant friends didn't: her mother spoke English well. Heejae's mother was a fierce advocate for her at school. She also translated for the parents of her friends.[8]

Following business school at Stanford University, Heejae decided to do what she does best: address a difficult problem using her advanced technology know-how. She founded TalkingPoints as a nonprofit to translate messages between teachers and parents.

About a quarter of all school children in the United States speak a language other than English at home. These are families where parents often work multiple jobs, may come from cultures where parents are not supposed to engage with teachers, and most importantly, do not speak English well enough to feel comfortable speaking to teachers.

Family engagement with schools is not a minor issue when it comes to educational outcomes. It is twice as effective in predicting school success than socioeconomic status. Let that sink in for a second: for school success matters much less whether a child is from a high-income home than whether adults in a child's life talk to their teachers. However, family-school engagement occurs up to 50% *less* among families in under-resourced, multilingual communities.[9]

TalkingPoints' app works like text messaging on mobile devices. It operates in over 100 languages, provides closed captioning for video messages for parents who may not be comfortable writing, and enables parents and guardians to engage with teachers during the cracks of their very busy days.

TalkingPoints started with a simple proof of concept and a small group of families. Using a Google spreadsheet, a text messaging app, and human translators, Heejae and her team simulated an automated process from end to end. Here's how it worked. A parent sent a text message in their native language. Heejae added it to the spreadsheet. Next, a human translator translated the message into English. Heejae texted the translated message to the teacher or administrator. And back and forth they went. Heejae told us, "We always start with a proof of concept with a small group before we build, as part of doing no harm."

The team learned a lot from this early testing and automated and launched the pilot version in 2015 with 100 families. Most importantly, they learned they couldn't rely on off-the-shelf translation tools alone because these tools often misinterpreted context and cultural norms. The volunteer translators review the machine translation to ensure cultural accuracy and that educational terms are accurately translated. These translations are being fed back into the model to continuously improve it. The aim is to build a large and deep enough database of translations to direct only the difficult-to-understand conversations to human translators.

TalkingPoints meets our definition of smart nonprofits: organizations that are human-centered, prepared, and knowledgeable and reflective. People are deeply engaged in the process, and the team designed and are implementing the app carefully and thoughtfully; they have done their homework about cultural competence, education, and the needs of immigrant families; the staff includes people with experts in education and tech; and everyone has experience working with immigrant families and schools.

The results show the effectiveness of working this way.

By 2019, the app facilitated over 20 million conversations for 500,000 parents and teachers. TalkingPoints is also free for users. An outside research firm was engaged to evaluate the effort. It found that:

- 89% of the schools using the app serve low-income children.
- 97% of teachers have found TalkingPoints helpful in meeting their family engagement goals.
- 98% of teachers were able to reach families they had never reached before.
- 83% of teachers believe that they are more informed about students' needs because of their relationships with families.[10]

VI-SPDAT blocked access to services. TalkingPoints creates access for a woefully underserved population. These cases highlight why it is so important for organizations to step carefully into the use of smart tech.

THE DANGERS OF AUTOMATION

Nicholas Carr wrote in *The Glass Cage*, "Automation severs ends from means. It makes getting what we want easier, but it distances us from the work of knowing."[11]

There is enormous danger and damage to be done in distancing ourselves from knowing. It means potentially cutting ourselves off from the needs of clients if they are first interacting with bots screening them for services. It could mean using automation to send out many times more fundraising appeals and not listening to the complaints from current and prospective donors. It could mean hiding behind screens instead of stepping out to build stronger relationships with constituents. And it could mean allowing an insidious form of racism and sexism to take hold unabated inside your organization.

We tend to see work done by computers and robots as incapable of being swayed by emotions and therefore incapable of being racist, sexist, or otherwise biased or unfair. However, the code that powers smart tech was at some point created by people and carries forward their opinions, assumptions, and biases. When this code makes decisions that are discriminatory, we call it *embedded bias*. The renowned data scientist Cathy O'Neil says, "Algorithms are opinions embedded in code."[12]

Embedded biases are very difficult to undo. Programmers make literally thousands of choices beneath the hood of smart tech that the rest of us can't see. Automation is increasingly being used to make vital and life-changing decisions for people. Therefore, the choices that programmers (overwhelmingly white men) make, based on their own experiences and backgrounds, become more important.

For instance, smart tech is increasingly used to screen applications for mortgages. It is illegal to ask questions about, say, race, in these applications, so programmers create "proxies," or substitute questions, to create a profile of an applicant. For instance, a zip code could be used as a proxy for "safe neighborhood." Safe generally means white, particularly for white programmers using their own life experiences. In addition, the data is needed to train smart tech systems. An automated mortgage screening process will use data from the enormous data sets from past mortgage application decisions. Black people were historically denied mortgages at astonishing rates and therefore will be woefully underrepresented in these data sets. In this way, seemingly benign programming decisions, mundane proxies, and historic data create embedded biases against people of color that is difficult to see from the outside.

Once bias is baked into smart tech, it stays there forever and becomes self-reinforcing over time. Nancy Smyth, former dean of the School of Social Work at the University of Buffalo, State University of New York, says, "Code is racist because society is racist."[13]

In her book *Race After Technology*, Ruha Benjamin describes a "New Jim Code." It is a take on the old Jim Crow that powered decades of institutional racism in Reconstructionist southern states. She writes, "The animating force of the New Jim Code is that tech designers encode judgments into technical systems but claim that the racist results of their designs are entirely exterior to the encoding process. Racism thus becomes doubled—magnified and buried under layers of digital denial."[14] She later writes, ". . . the outsourcing of human decisions is, at once, the insourcing of coded inequity." We will explore the ethical use of smart tech throughout this book.

About This Book

The book is divided into three parts. Part I, "Understanding and Using Artificial Intelligence," focuses on the leadership needed to use smart tech well, the history of smart tech, and key issues for using it that organizations need to be prepared for: the need to stay deeply human-centered in planning and use of smart tech, the enormous amounts of clean data necessary to power the systems, and the ethical concerns and considerations necessary to ensure bias is mitigated.

Part II, "The Smart Nonprofit: Use-Case Examples and Management," focuses on the applications of smart tech within organizations. It begins with a chapter to carefully and thoughtfully select a specific application of smart tech. Chapters on the use of smart tech for program delivery, fundraising, back-office operations, and philanthropy follow.

Part III, "Where We Go from Here," concludes with a look about the probable future of nonprofits and social change in an automated world.

Conclusion

We wrote this book to help organizations prepare to benefit from automation and avoid mistakes. Smart tech can help nonprofits become more efficient and use that dividend of time to build better relationships with stakeholders inside and outside of the organization. Smart tech can better leverage data to better understand program impact. We want nonprofits to harness this technology for good, which requires organizational leaders to understand the limitations of smart tech and apply it strategically, ethically, and with responsibility.

Ultimately, the purpose of using smart tech shouldn't be to make organizations go faster but to make your organization better at solving problems and taking care of people inside and outside in more humane ways. This will only happen when everyone in the organization has the information, tools, and opportunity to shape their own lives and futures. That's the true mark of success for a smart nonprofit and what we will share in the rest of the book.

Endnotes

1. Sydney Brownstone, "This data tool helps homeless people get housing. If you're white, your chances are even better," *The Seattle Times* (October 29, 2019), https://www.seattletimes.com/seattle-news/homeless/this-data-tool-helps-homeless-people-get-housing-if-youre-white-your-chances-are-even-better/.
2. Leah Post, author email interview on July 9, 2021.

3. Heather L. McCauley, ScD; Taylor Reid, BA, Michigan State University, "Assessing Vulnerability, Prioritizing Risk: The Limitations of the VI-SPDAT for Survivors of Domestic & Sexual Violence" (July 20, 2020), https://dcadv.org/file_download/inline/b1bb3b28-8039-4590-aa1d-daaef5fb6546.

4. Iain De Jong, author interview on June 25, 2021.

5. Jake Maguire, author interview on June 30, 2021.

6. Steve MacLaughlin, "The Impact of AI on Philanthropy" *Engage Podcast Series* (October 20, 2020), https://nofilternonprofit.blackbaud.com/raise-engage-podcast-series/episode-167-the-impact-of-ai-on-philanthropy.

7. Chris Arsenault, "Using AI, Canadian city predicts who might become homeless," *Reuters* (October 15, 2020), https://www.reuters.com/article/us-canada-homelessness-tech-idCAKBN27013Y.

8. Heejae Lim, author interview on August 4, 2021.

9. Google AI Impact Challenge (https://ai.google/social-good/impact-challenge/).

10. TalkingPoints website, https://talkingpts.org/talkingpoints-increases-parent-engagement-for-student-success/415/.

11. Nicholas Carr, *The Glass Cage* (New York: W. W. Norton & Company; September 8, 2015).

12. Cathy O'Neill, Naked Capitalism Blog, August 26, 2027, https://www.nakedcapitalism.com/2017/08/data-scientist-cathy-oneil-algorithms-opinions-embedded-code.html.

13. Nancy Smyth, author interview on May 25, 2021.

14. Ruha Benjamin, *Race After Technology* (New York: Wiley; June 17, 2019).

CHAPTER 2

Leading Smart Nonprofits

INTRODUCTION

Smart tech challenges our notions of power and autonomy, which is why blindly sliding into its use without adequate knowledge or preparation is such a frightening prospect. George Westerman wrote, "Technology changes quickly, but organizations change much more slowly. This . . . is the reason that digital transformation is more of a leadership challenge than a technical one."[1]

Our greatest concern is the possibility that leaders will think smart tech is a technical problem to be solved by the IT department rather than a profoundly important leadership issue. This is the pathway to the unethical use of smart tech. The careful and ethical use of smart tech within organizations isn't possible without engaged, thoughtful leadership.

No boards would hire executive directors who said finance wasn't for them, they didn't get it, and they would leave the budgeting and financial decisions up to other people. Fortunately, you do not need to become a computer programmer to understand how and why technology is changing your organization and the world. Smart tech is taking over decision-making in many parts of organizations, and senior leaders need to understand how this technology works and when and how to use it well. The people most affected by automation are the staff doing the everyday work of keeping organizations functioning: book-keepers, social workers, human resource professionals, and fund-raisers. They deserve to know what's happening and why and what the organization's plans are for automation. Leading the integration of smart tech into organizations begins by engaging in honest and open conversations with staff about the upcoming impact of automation on jobs. It is more than a mistake—it's a moral failure—to promise that no one will lose their job because of automation. A person charged with restocking the shelves in the food pantry is likely to be replaced by a robot soon. That doesn't mean that there may not be other tasks for this person to do. Good leadership means figuring this out together.

Organizational leaders need to continuously weigh the costs and benefits of automation. On one hand, smart tech offers superhuman capabilities to, say, predict cash flow, recommend language for emails to supporters, find prospective donors, answer common questions online, and much more that we will explore in this book. On the other hand, it raises a host of staffing and ethical issues that organizations will need to work through carefully. Everyone in your organization will be affected by auto-mation, and everyone, to some extent, needs to be involved in thinking about it and implementing it.

This chapter examines the leadership challenges of becoming a smart nonprofit, the impact smart tech will have on jobs and staffing, and the type of leadership necessary to ultimately reach the dividend of time. We'll begin with one of the biggest barriers to organizational change: the busyness paradox.

THE BUSYNESS PARADOX

Nonprofit workers have traditionally been underpaid and over-worked. The toxic combination of low pay and long hours leads to exhaustion, mistakes, and ultimately burnout. These factors are amplified by the always-on work culture created by digital tech. Email and text messages (and more recently work platforms such as Slack that combine the best and worst of email and text messages) never stop. The resulting cacophony makes it difficult to distinguish true crises from everyday work. Everything happens at once at operatically high volume.

Brigid Schulte calls this the "busyness paradox." She writes, "When we're busy and have that high-octane, panicked feeling that time is scarce . . . our attention and ability to focus narrows."[2]

Behavioral research has described this state as being in a tunnel because we are only able to concentrate on the most immediate, and often low-value, tasks. Other research has found we actually lose about 13 IQ points in this state.[3]

Many nonprofits are trapped in this endless cycle of busyness by responding to fire alarms, jumping from meeting to meeting, and batting back emails. We end our days feeling more overwhelmed, realizing that we haven't even started on the mission-critical and important tasks.

The busyness paradox is worse in nonprofits than commercial businesses because of the nature of the work. In 2011, major parts of the nonprofit sector were adamantly opposed to proposed federal government regulations requiring payment for overtime work. According to *The Atlantic*, "There's no doubt that nonprofits today face serious financial difficulties and constraints, but do they have no choice but to demand long, unpaid hours from their employees? Putting questions of fairness aside, is their treatment of their workers limiting their effectiveness?"[4]

The Urban Institute found that most nonprofits choose to cut salaries, benefits, and other costs long before scaling back their operations. "There is this feeling that the mission is so important that nothing should get in the way of it," Elizabeth T. Boris, one of the Urban Institute report's authors, says.[5]

Added to the problem of busyness is the nonprofit habit of continuing to offer and support outdated programs. It is common for organizations to add programs without eliminating any. This may happen because organizations are chasing funding that results in creating a new program rather than supporting an existing one. Or because it's painful to admit a program doesn't work. Whatever the reason, the resulting sideways growth adds to the frantic busyness of organizations trying to do too much, provide too many services, serve too many people and communities, and make more change in the world than their resources allow. Leaders—with staff and constituent input, of course—are responsible for not just what to do, but what *not* to do. The introduction of smart tech is an ideal moment to really dig into what organizations do and why they do it, get to the essence of their efforts, and determine what actions are most important for them to meet their missions. And get rid of everything else.

If smart tech is introduced into an organization that chooses to always be on, where every situation is a crisis, then the result will be amplifying the busyness paradox rather than undoing it.

CREATING HEALTHY CULTURES

Every organization has a set of cultural norms, or values, it uses to guide decision-making. They may be invisible and unspoken, but they are embedded in the DNA of the organization, or more specifically in the DNA of the leadership of the organization. These norms dictate whether an organization is open or closed, willing to accept feedback from staff and clients or dismissive of it, respectful of people's private time or invasive of it. This can all be summed up as "the way we do things around here."

Nonprofit workers come to their jobs because of an intense desire to make the world a better place. It is more than a job; it is a calling for many people. They are often willing to stick with it even when it's exhausting and the hours are long because they believe deeply in the mission. However, when the values they believe their organizations stand for, such as health and well-being, don't match up with the work, it can be soul crushing.

What organizations think their norms and values are and the everyday experience of people inside and outside are often very different. Your organization is "warm and welcoming" because it says so right there on the homepage of your website. And yet, the experience of constituents is that the literal and metaphoric doors are always closed. Or "we value our staff's mental and physical health," and yet we expect them to respond to emails at ten p.m. Automation is going to supersize these disconnects, unless leadership really digs into ensuring a healthy organizational culture.

We encourage organizations to have open discussions about their current culture and where and how it may not align with their values by using prompts like these:

- What do we value most as an organization? How and when can we see these values in practice? Do outsiders agree that these are our top values?

- Do we value our staff's privacy? For instance, do we expect people to always be reachable? And how do we use their data?

- How do our organizational values align with how we treat our staff and external stakeholders?

- When have we prioritized the needs and interests of our people and when have we not?

- What does it feel like when our organization is more interested in numbers than people?

- Are we accessible to the outside world? What data do we have that illustrates this?

- How do we make clients and other constituents feel known or unknown, heard or unheard, important or unimportant? How do we know they feel this way?

We cannot tell you the right answers for your organization. We can share the lessons we have learned working with many organizations over the years to help them create healthy work cultures.

One discussion is not enough. This is an ongoing conversation that needs to happen several times a year. There also need to be mechanisms in place for staff and constituents to be heard when these values aren't lived. If no human resources department exists, a trusted staff person, selected by all employees, can be designated as the keeper of the complaints to be shared with leadership. This makes leadership accountable for responding to issues.

Real data is needed to answer the questions. We have sat with executive directors who have data in their hands showing, say, how difficult it is for clients to reach a staff person and have them reject the findings outright. We appreciate that these conversations can be difficult and painful to have, particularly when the reality doesn't match people's hopes; however, everyone needs to trust and respond to real data. Data from staff and constituents needs to be collected and analyzed fearlessly and wholeheartedly to realign values with work.

No more excuses. You are busy. You are under-resourced. The work never stops. Yes, yes, yes. Smart tech isn't going to magically make these problems disappear. And you still need to do better. There are no excuses for treating people badly and making them feel small and invisible. Burnout is an incredibly expensive problem for organizations. It costs enormous amounts of time and money to replace workers, plus the disruption of losing institutional knowledge and perhaps beloved colleagues. It is a choice, and a very bad one, to allow toxic work cultures to fester.

Creating healthy cultures is the jumping-off point for dealing thoughtfully with the impact smart tech is going to have on jobs and work.

SMART TECH AND JOBS

There is enormous debate and disagreement on the effect smart tech will have on workers. The optimists believe that enormous job gains will occur from the integration of smart tech into organizations in areas such as data science and computer programming and even ethics (brush off those resumes, philosophy majors!).[6,7,8]

The pessimists believe smart tech is already reducing the humanity of workers. Not only is it dehumanizing to have people report to computers, it is widening the pay gap and providing no opportunity for advancement.[9]

Amazon, Uber, and Task Rabbit are companies in the "gig economy" that use workers as interchangeable cogs in their enormous systems. Gig economy companies hire people for a specific, narrow purpose. It is estimated that fifty-five million people in the United States are gig workers.[10]

The benefits for gig workers are flexibility about when and for how long they want to work and instant cash. They also get low pay, the loneliness of not having any colleagues, a lack of benefits, and no union; and they are supervised by bots instead of people through constant surveillance, lack transparency about how jobs are allocated, and lack any human engagement with the mother ship. These jobs have become cautionary tales about the creation of two classes of workers—the managers of algorithms and workers managed by algorithms. Gig workers are treated similarly to the millions of computer servers Google uses. Gig companies don't fix any broken ones; they just buy new ones.[11]

There is the potential for workers in, say, childcare or after-school tutoring, to turn into gigs, meaning they will be part-time freelancers (to save on benefits) who are available for shifts and report to bots, not people. This will happen when budgets are more important than people. The way out of this trap is to focus on creating healthy organizational cultures to ensure people always come first. Healthy cultures create healthy work environments that create good jobs.

And then there are the Solomonic prognosticators like the World Economic Forum that split the difference by saying jobs will be lost due to automation, but many more new ones will be created.

Bots aren't just replacing jobs people want to do; they're also replacing jobs people shouldn't have to do. From Wikipedia, "Physical robots are highly desired in many industries, especially to perform tasks often referred to as the four 'D's."[12] And Kathleen Walch writes in *Forbes*, "These robots operate every day in manufacturing, warehouse, health care, and other situations to perform the tasks that would otherwise be performed by humans with not always positive outcomes."[13]

Based on our research and discussions with experts around the world, our conclusion is that no one knows for sure whether the net change will be jobs gained or lost, but the tasks people do every day will undoubtedly change. According to recent research by McKinsey & Company on the future of work, the foundational employee skills needed in an era of automation include:

- Add value beyond what can be done by automated systems and intelligent machines.

- Operate in a digital environment.

- Continually adapt to new ways of working and new occupations.[14]

If you took a poll of nonprofit workers and asked them who came into this work to operate in a digital environment or continually adapt to new ways of working, it's unlikely very many hands would go up.

The widespread use of smart tech carries with it centuries of fears about when and how machines will replace workers. A survey of more than 1200 managers responded to this question: What are the barriers to your team adapting to new technology? The top response was resistance to change (43%).[15] Working through this resistance carefully and empathetically is the chief challenge for leadership of smart nonprofits.

LEADING THROUGH RESISTANCE

Most people are resistant to technological changes at work. They fear having to learn new skills, feeling inexpert, losing power and status, and, of course, losing their jobs. These fears are not the sole purview of frontline workers. People everywhere on the organizational chart, up and down and side to side, have these concerns, and this is not a new phenomenon.

Dr. Harvey Cushing witnessed a demonstration of the sphygmomanometer, or blood pressure cuff, at a hospital in Italy in 1901. He enthusiastically brought the device back to Johns Hopkins Hospital in Baltimore where he expected an enthusiastic greeting. Instead it was roundly rejected by his colleagues. Technically, the device was a success; it provided a standard measure of the pressure required to obliterate the flow of blood in a patient's arm. However, it also threatened the expertise of physicians and that was unacceptable to his colleagues.

Physicians were trained to assess the flow of blood through touch, or palpation. It took years to hone this skill and mastering it was a source of pride and professionalism for doctors. The problem wasn't instrumentation, per se. Stopwatches and thermometers were regularly used to gather and record health data but only by doctors. Cushing's tool allowed anyone, even, dare we say, a nurse, to wrap the cuff around an arm and write down the results.

It took ten years for the blood pressure cuff to replace palpation and become a standard part of medical care by physicians. But not by itself. The standard of care became the use of the blood pressure cuff in conjunction with the stethoscope to enable physicians to listen to blood flow. This kept the practice of assessing blood flow firmly within the purview of physicians. It took another forty years before nurses were allowed to perform these functions, at first using their pastel-colored "assistoscopes" rather than the "real" stethoscopes.

In the end, finally, the blood pressure cuff takes standard, accurate measurements of blood circulation, and the professionals use the data as one factor in their overall assessment of the health of a patient.[16]

This is not just the story of the resistance by experts to one medical device; it is the story of the resistance by experts to *all* technological changes throughout history. The wheel replaced our legs, the printing press replaced handwriting, and Wikipedia replaced the set of Encyclopedia Britannica on our shelves. The introduction of the industrial loom created such a backlash from expert weavers that they burned down the factories. These were the Luddites, named after Ned Ludd, a young apprentice who was rumored to have wrecked a textile apparatus in 1779. These people became the everlasting symbol for technological resistance. They were concerned that the industrial loom threatened their status, their expertise, and their livelihoods. And they were right. Weaving machines did put many artisans out of work. However, it also created many more jobs for low-skilled workers and a new middle class.[17]

Working through resistance takes time and patience, but it is much better and smarter in the long run to carefully and consciously put in the effort. Without smart leadership, the fears and concerns won't go away; they'll just fester and feed a toxic workplace. Leading organizations through technological change requires being:

Trustworthy. Replacing humans with machines requires a leap of faith that human beings will retain their usefulness and relevance to the organization. Of course, transparency helps, but it's not enough because being see-through is not the same as being trustworthy.

Recently, an executive director said to us, "Who needs a five-person fundraising team when bots are going to do the research and communications automatically?" We could see budget calculations scrolling through his brain. A cost-saving possibility for him is a terrifying reality for his staff. We felt bad for the staff of that organization led by someone more interested in the budget than their livelihoods.

The essence of trust is believing that someone is there to help you, that they have your back in good and bad times. Automating organizational tasks or functions without preparing people is a very fast way to make your organization feel untrustworthy inside and out. Imagine you are a client used to talking to a social worker about various benefits and how to apply for them, and now you are told to talk to a screen? Or you're a bookkeeper and now new software is doing most of your work. How would these changes make you feel? How would it make other staff members watching these changes feel?

It's important to be very careful about what you are promising in this next phase of organizational develop-ment. For instance, if you say a person will always be available to answer questions, and they aren't, trust will be lost. Clear, open, honest communication with internal and external stakeholders is critically important to ensure that fears and gossip aren't allowed to take hold.

And remember, you and your organization are being watched all day, every day, online. Your reputation is being tracked on websites like Glassdoor. You cannot afford a trust gap between what you say you are and how your organization shows up in the world.

Empathetic. Leaders need to stay carefully attuned to stakeholder feelings about changes brought about by smart tech. It may be tempting to change a development staffer's job from 80% research to 80% relationship building with potential donors. Now, right away. However, this is not only cruel to that staff person but also unlikely to work well if the staff person is either uninterested or unable to make that change. Here are the particular areas where empathetic leadership is needed most:

- *The Introduction of Smart Tech:* Replacing people with machines is a huge organizational change. Everyone affected needs a chance to learn about what it is and isn't, to have their questions answered about how their roles will change and how the organization will stay attuned to the impact those changes are having on staff and clients. Patience is required for the time this will take, but it is time well spent if it avoids hidden resistance in the future.

- *Employee Support:* Jobs are going to change, and this is going to be painful for many people. Having honest discussions with staff about changes to their roles and responsibilities and providing coaching and support are not only smart ways to work but humane ways to lead. Ultimately, this new job may not be for her, but maybe there is some other role for her. Perhaps she can receive training as a data scientist. People deserve a chance to flex old muscles or gain new skills without constantly fearing they are about to be fired.

- *Getting Real Feedback:* Organizations led by people who are too brittle or uninterested in real feedback cannot learn and improve. Empathetic leaders want to know how the changes feel to staff and constituents. They want to know whether the organization is staying human-centric, and how they as leaders can improve.

Curious. We are in the very beginning of a revolution in the way organizations are structured and operate. There will be many more ways that machines are making decisions and doing the work that only people can do today.

Successfully navigating these changes requires leaders who are willing to learn and adapt throughout their careers.

We often hear older people talk about "digital natives," meaning younger people who never knew a life before iPhones and iPads. Those natives have a natural affinity for digital tech in ways many older people find confounding. This is true *and* a convenient excuse for outsourcing tech knowledge. Smart tech is too important to the core operations of organizations for leaders to turn over decision-making to someone else. Leaders need to stay engaged, open, and curious about how smart tech works and how it is changing internal operations and workplace culture.

Here are ways to stay curious about smart tech:

- Organize or attend monthly meetings to explore what's new in smart tech that can help your organization succeed. Smart tech is going to continue to expand and grow quickly. It is vitally important to stay up-to-date on the ways the tech can be used to improve your organization's efforts.

- Think about smart tech "experiments." Identify a particular use for smart tech within your organization and give it a try for, say, three months. Reflect on what went well and what didn't, and try it again. Think of this as an ongoing process of exploration and discovery.

- Explore your organization's efforts from the outside in. Too many organizations get trapped into thinking they understand how well they are doing, how it feels to be a client or donor or volunteer, from the inside out. It is critically important to take your organization for a test run as a constituent. Make a donation and experience the thank-you process yourself. Sign up for a service, and experience your organization from the perspective of a client. This will not only expand your empathy for stakeholders but enable you to imagine different ways of working.

CONCLUSION

Smart tech can be a catalyst for rethinking organizational life and ensuring that people inside and out are treated with dignity and respect, with the right kind of leadership in place to usher it in carefully and thoughtfully. Mistakes will be made by people trying to do good things; resistance may pop up in unexpected places and even from surprising people. Leadership ensures that everyone keeps rowing together in the same direction.

ENDNOTES

1. George Westerman, "The First Law of Digital Inclusion" (April 08, 2019), https://sloanreview.mit.edu/article/the-first-law-of-digital-innovation/.
2. Brigid Schulte, "Preventing Busyness from Becoming Burnout," *Harvard Business Review* (April 15, 2019), https://hbr.org/2019/04/preventing-busyness-from-becoming-burnout.
3. Sendhil Mullainathan and Eldar Shafir, "Freeing Up Intelligence," *Scientific American Mind* (February, 2014), https://scholar.harvard.edu/files/sendhil/files/scientificamericanmind0114-58.pdf.
4. Jonathan Timm, "The Plight of the Overworked Employee," *The Atlantic* (August 24, 2016), https://www.theatlantic.com/business/archive/2016/08/the-plight-of-the-overworked-nonprofit-employee/497081/.
5. Sarah L. Pettijohn and Elizabeth T. Boris with Carol J. De Vita and Saunji D. Fyffe, "Nonprofit-Government Contracts and

Grants: Findings from the 2013 National Survey," Urban Institute, (December 2013), https://www.urban.org/sites/default/files/publication/24231/412962-Nonprofit-Government-Contracts-and-Grants-Findings-from-the-National-Survey.PDF.

6. Beyond Limits, "Why Artificial Intelligence Is Poised To Create More Jobs," https://www.beyond.ai/news/artificial-intelligence-creates-more-jobs/.

7. Thomas W. Malone, Daniela Rus, and Robert Laubacher, "Artificial Intelligence and the Future of Work," MIT Center For Collective Intelligence, Research Brief 17 (December, 2020), https://workofthefuture.mit.edu/wp-content/uploads/2020/12/2020-Research-Brief-Malone-Rus-Laubacher2.pdf.

8. WIRED Brand Lab for Accenture, AI and the Future of Work, *Wired Magazine* (April, 2018), https://www.wired.com/wiredinsider/2018/04/ai-future-work/.

9. Mike Walsh, "Algorithms Are Making Economic Inequality Worse," *Harvard Business Review* (October 22, 2020), https://hbr.org/2020/10/algorithms-are-making-economic-inequality-worse.

10. Nandita Bose "U.S. Labor Secretary supports classifying gig workers as employees," Reuters (April 29, 2021), https://www.reuters.com/world/us/exclusive-us-labor-secretary-says-most-gig-workers-should-be-classified-2021-04-29/.

11. Mareike Möhlmann and Ola Henfridsson, "What People Hate About Being Managed by Algorithms, According to a Study of Uber Drivers," *Harvard Business Review* (August 30, 2019), https://hbr.org/2019/08/what-people-hate-about-being-managed-by-algorithms-according-to-a-study-of-uber-drivers.

12. Wikipedia entry, "Dirty, dangerous and demeaning," https://en.wikipedia.org/wiki/Dirty,_dangerous_and_demeaning, last accessed August 7, 2021.

13. Kathleen Walch, "You've Heard of Robots; What Are Cobots," *Forbes* (December 15, 2019), https://www.forbes.com/sites/cognitiveworld/2019/12/15/youve-heard-of-robots-what-are-cobots/?sh=815248b48626.

14. Marco Dondi, Julia Klier, Frédéric Panier, and Jörg Schubert, "Defining the skills citizens will need in the future world of work," McKinsey (June 25, 2021), https://www.mckinsey.com/Industries/Public-and-Social-Sector/Our-Insights/Defining-the-skills-citizens-will-need-in-the-future-world-of-work.

15. Robert Half, "Jobs & AI Anxiety," https://www.roberthalf.com/sites/default/files/documents_not_indexed/RH_Future-of-Work19.pdf (2019).

16. Christopher W. Crenne, MD, PhD, "Introduction of the Blood Pressure Cuff into U.S. Medical Practice: Technology and Skilled Practice," *Annals of Internal Medicine* (March 15, 1998), https://www.acpjournals.org/doi/pdf/10.7326/0003-4819-128-6-199803150-00010.

17. "Marching with 'General Ludd': Machine Breaking in the Industrial Revolution," Congressional Rights Foundation, https://www.crf-usa.org/bill-of-rights-in-action/bria-17-2-b-marching-with-general-ludd-machine-breaking-in-the-industrial-revolution.

CHAPTER 3

The Evolution of Smart Tech

INTRODUCTION

Advanced digital technology took decades of research and development, testing, iterating, failure, and finally commercializing the technology for it to become commonplace today. Its seemingly sudden arrival for end users can feel startling and frightening.

We have been here before technologically. Calestous Juma writes, "There has been ongoing societal tension between the need for innovation and pressure to maintain continuity, social order and stability throughout human history."[1] For hundreds of years, we have created tools to make work faster and easier, safer, and more efficient. From the printing press to telephones to mainframe and then desktop computers, each generation has made life and work easier. However, those tools weren't "smart"; they didn't make decisions for people and decide, say, who receives services and who doesn't.

This chapter provides an overview of the history and development of smart tech, an explanation of how it works, and its applications for the field of social good, which enables us to understand how best to use it now. We also cover important emerging trends as smart tech becomes ubiquitous.

A Brief History

The history of smart tech begins at the Dartmouth Workshop in 1954. John McCarthy, a computer science professor at Dartmouth College, coined the phrase in his grant proposal to the Rockefeller Foundation to support the workshop. He wrote: "Every feature of intelligence can be precisely described so that a machine can be made to simulate it. An attempt will be made to find how to make machines use language, form abstractions and concepts, solve all kinds of problems now reserved for humans, and improve themselves."[2]

Over the next six decades, artificial intelligence grew into a complex computer science field with an alphabet soup of technical jargon and many different subspecialities. There was an occasional burst of public displays of smart tech wizardry as when IBM's Deep Blue computer beat the world's best chess player, Garry Kasparov, in their second match in 1997. For the most part, the public view of the field was led by science fiction writers such as Isaac Asimov and pop culture with either a utopian view like the Jetsons or more likely a dystopian story of killer robots.

The rise of the internet in the early 1990s began to turn science fiction into reality. In 1965, Gordon E. Moore, the founder of the computer chip manufacturing company Intel, predicted that the computational power of a single chip would double every two years. This became known as Moore's law and not only did it come true, it changed the world of computing, meaning the world. It also underestimated how much more powerful computers would become in the next several decades. The exponential increase in the power of computers and decrease in their size ensured that everyday people would eventually hold phones that were more powerful than entire rooms of mainframe computers in the 1970s.

The internet began to be commercially available in the early 1990s. We could connect and communicate with people in the next cubicle or across the world. And soon, we were sharing and storing photos and information. And then came Big Tech. These are companies that provided the infrastructure for our use of digital technology: internet service providers such as AOL initially and eventually AT&T and Comcast, web browsers such as Chrome and Firefox, search companies like Google, and social media companies like Facebook and Twitter. It all seemed miraculous and free. And then we realized Big Tech owned all of our data and they were gleefully selling it for enormous profits. This was a wake-up call that we really needed to be aware of ethics as we deal with technology.

Now smart tech is becoming ubiquitous, and what was once unimaginable science fiction like speaking into your wristwatch or sending information around the world in an instant has become our everyday reality. And we're just about to do it again. As the technologist Clay Shirky wrote, "Digital tools don't get socially interesting until they get technologically boring."[3]

Smart tech is about to get boring.

Here's how the technology works. Programmers use computer code to create algorithms, the rules for analyzing data and making predictions, suggestions, or automated completion of tasks such as reviewing applications, or resumes. The predictions algorithms make about what people will do or want are what we humans call decision-making. This isn't one decision; algorithms make millions of calculations in the blink of an eye, and we can't see any of it happen.

It takes almost unimaginably enormous amounts of data to train smart tech systems to identify these patterns and then huge amounts of data to make the systems work thereafter.

Once implemented, smart tech isn't done learning. It continues honing its decision-making and becomes smarter over time.

Using a baking analogy, computer codes are the ingredients, algorithms are the recipes, and decisions are the cakes.

Smart tech has recently reached an inflection point common to technologies that reach everyday use: an enormous increase in computing power meets a dramatic decrease in the cost of the technology. As a result, technology that was previously available only to elite institutions like NASA or embedded in widely complicated systems such as airplanes (autopilots) or smartphones (autocorrect) has suddenly become available to everyday people and organizations.

DIGITAL ERAS AND DISRUPTIVE TECHNOLOGY

Jeremiah Owyang, a leading technology analyst, outlines six digital eras.[4] They are:

- *Internet Era:* Organizations' biggest challenge was digitizing information from the physical world.

- *Social Media Era:* Invisible networks from the physical world become digital and visible and scalable. Organizations shift their approaches to fundraising and communications because people have access to much more information and can support many more causes. Activism, engagement, and ideas spread faster due to the network effect.

- *Collaborative Economy Era:* People can share resources with each other. Uber and Airbnb are common examples. Crowdfunding efforts, particularly platforms like GoFundMe, democratize fundraising by and for individuals.

- *Autonomous World Era:* New technologies such as artificial intelligence, machine learning, and chatbots analyze data faster than ever, and human tasks are automated. This era is emerging, and early adopters are applying autonomous tech in pilot projects.

- *Modern Well-Being Era:* We turn to technology to become more human. This includes wellness apps and avoiding or rehabbing from technology addiction and overload.

- *Off Planet Era:* Leaving Earth becomes possible for civilians, and everyone has opportunities to have God's view.

Each of these eras includes disruptive technologies that force a rethinking of existing business models and practices, and they are overlapping as we are still in the internet, social media, and collaborative economy eras. This book focuses on the autonomous world. We will leave the discussion of how we will adapt to living on Mars for a future book.

ACCELERATING INTO THE AUTONOMOUS WORLD

Right now, we are hitting the sweet spot for smart tech when the cost of technology declines and the commercial availability of it increases. These moments of technology adoption are often drawn in the shape of a hockey stick. The blade of the stick moves slowly along the bottom of the graph until the technology becomes inexpensive and useful enough to the public that adoption explodes upward and becomes the handle of the stick.

Here are just a few data points that illustrate the acceleration:

- Since 1997, the number of published papers has increased nine times.

- Patents for AI appeared in 9% of technologies in 1976, spreading to more than 42% of technologies by 2018.

- The number of startups using AI has increased fourteen-fold since 2000.[5,6]

KEY ASPECTS OF THE AUTONOMOUS WORLD

The autonomous world covers a wide variety of technologies. For instance, artificial intelligence is divided into three broad types: narrow (focusing on a narrowly defined task); general (as capable as a human), and super (more capable than a human). General and super AI are used in more academic and experimental settings right now.

Our purpose for this book is to focus on the most important smart tech applications for social change efforts today and in the near future. Therefore, most of the examples in this book are narrow AI involving machine learning and conversational artificial intelligence (the ability for computers and humans to communicate via text or voice). Rest assured that smart tech is not smarter than people (yet). We will discuss the differences between human and machine intelligence in Chapter 4, "Staying Human-Centered."

Machine Learning

Machine learning automates specific tasks through pattern matching. This is how children learn languages. They see a picture of an apple and repeat the word, then learn to read the word, and then learn to spell the world. Over and over again. Smart tech does this using much more data and going faster than people. Many current commercial applications use machine learning technology.[7]

Here's a lighthearted example of machine learning from Ben Hamm, an Amazon product manager. In order to stop his "sweet, murderous cat," Metric, from bringing dead animals into the house, Ben connected the cat flap in his door to a smart tech-enabled camera outside. The camera controlled the automated locking system for the cat door. Ben loaded photos of the cat with and without prey in his mouth to train the system to answer a simple question: "Is the cat coming into the house with dead prey in his mouth?" If the answer was yes, the cat flap locked for 15 minutes. In addition, it would automatically send a donation, or "blood money," to the National Audubon Society, which protects the birds that Metric loved to kill. If it answered no, the cat flap door would open and allow the prey-less cat entry into the house.[8]

In machine learning examples like this one, the data is purposely categorized and labeled to enable the system to recognize patterns. This is called "supervised learning," where data is labeled by humans and then the algorithm learns from training to make predictions. Programmers then adjust the algorithm to make correct predictions. For example, a supervised learning model can predict how long your commute will be based on the time of day, weather conditions, and so on. But first, you'll have to train it to know that rainy weather extends the driving time.

Unsupervised learning models, in contrast, work on their own to discover the inherent structure of unlabeled data. Note that they still require some human intervention to make sure the results are accurate. For example, an unsupervised learning model might detect a pattern whereby online shoppers who purchase baby clothing also buy other baby products. This would be very valuable information for advertisers to know.

Training smart tech systems to correctly identify and label images takes an enormous amount of time and data and, still, the results are often wrong. In 2017, a fun internet meme showed that a smart tech system couldn't tell the difference between blueberry muffins and chihuahuas.[9]

Two years later, in a more rigorous study conducted by a group of researchers from UC Berkeley, the University of Washington, and the University of Chicago, a machine learning algorithm thought a nail was a candle and a hummingbird was a snail. The researchers found "deep flaws" that stem from the software's "over-reliance on color, texture, and background cues."[10]

We will explore the need for large, clean data sets more in Chapter 5, "Data, Data, Data."

Conversational Artificial Intelligence

ELIZA made her debut in 1964. She was a voice-activated system simulating a psychotherapist trained to reply to questions with open-ended responses. Instead of paying an enormous amount of money to have a human therapist *not* answer your question, ELIZA was available at any time for free. ELIZA was the first conversational artificial intelligence to be claimed by some to pass the Turing Test (although this view is highly contentious), named after the computer scientist Alan Turing, which measures a machine's ability to exhibit intelligent behavior that is equivalent to that of humans.[11]

Natural-language programming collects and analyzes what's called *unstructured data*. These are huge amounts of data from, say, social media, organized by theme and sentiment to help guide communication decision-making. Alexa and Siri use natural-language programming to learn to understand both the content and purpose of questions. Chatbots are the fastest growing commercial use of natural-language programming. You may have engaged with a chatbot without knowing it. If you clicked on a button on a commercial site that says "Chat 24/7," chances are these are conversational chatbots programmed to answer rote questions. Chatbots will likely be the first smart tech tools that smaller nonprofit organizations can program by themselves. There are many examples of chatbots used to interact with donors and volunteers throughout this book, and we will share the lessons learned and best practices for adoption.

AI4Good

For the last decade, AI has been used extensively in support of humanitarian causes. Humanitarian crises that are transnational and generate enormous amounts of data are perfect places for the use of smart tech. This field is known as AI for Good (AI4Good). The main players are large nonprofit organizations in partnership with universities, international development agencies, healthcare, and large tech companies.[12]

In 2018, Google announced the AI Impact Challenge, an open call for proposals on how to use artificial intelligence (AI) to help address society's most pressing issues. Twenty organizations received a total of $25 million in grant funding. They received an enormous number of submissions, 2602 in total, from six continents. Their final report on the challenge identified subject areas for submissions as crisis response, economic empowerment, education, environment, equality and inclusion, health, and the public sector.[13]

These are all important areas to be addressed in the world, but we want to focus on three very active areas in the field of AI4Good: climate change, refugee management, and epidemiology and medical diagnoses.

Climate Change

In 2019, a group of well-known scientists and AI researchers published a paper called "Tackling Climate Change with Machine Learning."[14] It was a call to action bringing smart tech researchers and climate change scientists together to identify ways that the smart tech can help address climate change.

The researchers identified different examples where machine learning can be deployed, including energy production, carbon dioxide (CO_2) removal, education, solar geoengineering, and finance. Additional possibilities include more energy-efficient buildings, creating new low-carbon materials, better monitoring of deforestation, and greener transportation. However, despite the potential, the researchers point out that this is early days and AI isn't magic, although machine learning can help bring new insights into the problem of climate change.

Smart tech can unlock new insights from the massive amounts of data embedded in differing climate model simulations. For example, algorithms that analyze data from 30 climate models can improve predictions and can help governments make informed climate policy and prepare for change and potentially uncover areas that could reverse some effects of climate change.

Humans are not the only ones at risk because of climate change, of course. Planet Labs, an Earth-imaging tech company, partnered with Paul G. Allen Philanthropies and leading research scientists to create a global map to monitor the health of shallow-water coral reefs.[15]

These are examples of how smart tech is helping with climate change, but what about the environmental impact of the technology? Much of smart tech's recent adoption has required ever-increasing amounts of data and computing power, and this all comes at a cost. While currently cloud computing represents roughly 0.5% of the world's energy consumption, that percentage is projected to grow beyond 2% in the coming years.[16] The machine learning carbon emissions calculator helps individual users of machine learning to track their carbon emissions.[17]

Recommending greener machine learning technology and processes should be a key part of the technology's research and development process.

Refugee Crisis

There are an estimated 84 million forcibly displaced people and 26 million refugees worldwide, the highest numbers on record.[18] The pandemic combined with extreme weather events caused by climate change are exacerbating the challenges for humanitarian agencies to help refugees. The Hive, the innovations lab for the United Nation's High Commission on Refugees, has been leading efforts to introduce smart tech to support its program delivery. The Hive has partnered with Microsoft Philanthropies to identify and expand research opportunities where AI could be applied in the global refugee crisis.

In 2018, the Hive piloted a smart tech project to address the global problem of extreme overcrowding in refugee camps. For instance, Malawi's Dzaleka refugee camp, created in 1994 to house 9000 refugees from Rwanda and the Democratic Republic of Congo, today houses 30,000 refugees.

Monitoring camps for empty beds is an essential but labor-intensive activity, as field staff members typically survey the camps on the ground and upload the data manually. During the pandemic, this activity posed additional risk for staff.[19] The Hive joined forces with Maxar Technologies and Stanford University's Sustainability and Artificial Intelligence Lab to map and analyze refugee camp populations by using satellite imagery in real time.

They currently monitor 115 refugee camps and help local agencies steer refugees to camps with available beds.[20]

Using mapping data to pinpoint areas for humanitarian aid is critically important. However, many of the world's disaster-affected areas are literally missing from existing maps, making it difficult for humanitarian aid workers to prepare and deliver relief programs. To address this issue, Humanitarian OpenStreetMap Team (HOT) partnered with Microsoft and Bing to improve the mapping of areas vulnerable to natural disaster and poverty.[21]

Epidemiology and Diagnostics

Going viral took on a whole new meaning in 2020. In addition to news and memes, COVID-19 made its way from Wuhan, China, around the world in just days, not months or years. The pandemic demonstrated how vulnerable the world is to diseases, which pay no attention to national borders. Smart tech has been used to track the spread of the disease by epidemiologists, policy makers, and journalists. Smart tech can instantly translate health data into multiple languages.[22]

COVID-19 was also a vivid example of the different ways that countries around the world view privacy and smart tech. South Korea used geolocation data, surveillance-camera footage, and credit card records to trace COVID-19 patients. China assigned a risk level color (red, yellow, green) to each person indicating contagion risk using software embedded in individual cell phones. Austria, China, Israel, Poland, and Singapore set up contact tracing systems to identify possible infection routes. The use of facial recognition software for contact tracing in the United States immediately raised ethical issues of racial bias, inaccuracies, and privacy concerns. IBM and Apple soon suspended its use of facial recognition software indefinitely.[23]

Since so much of diagnoses rely on images and pattern matching, it is a perfect area for machine learning applications. Oncologists are using smart tech to diagnose a wide variety of cancers.[24] Researchers at the University of Heidelberg and Stanford University created a smart tech system to visually diagnose images of skin lesions to determine whether they were cancerous. It outperformed dozens of dermatologists.[25]

Smart tech can also help detect public health problems that are not visible. In fact they may even be hidden below ground. After lead was found in the pipes for drinking water in Flint, Michigan, smart tech was used to search underground pipes for lead. A machine learning model was used to predict which homes were most likely to have lead pipes. In 2017, workers inspected 8833 homes, and of those, 6228 homes had their pipes replaced—a 70% rate of accuracy. In 2018, 10,531 properties were explored and only 1567 of those were found to have lead pipes to replace. That's a lead pipe hit rate of just 15%. Why the dramatic drop in accuracy? Public officials abandoned science and began randomly digging up pipes across the city based on who complained the loudest. Hysteria won over science in Flint.[26,27]

Data4Good

A subset of AI4Good is the burgeoning field of Data for Good (Data4Good). The Data4Good field had its roots in 2002, when U2's Bono and a group of social entrepreneurs, anti-poverty activists, and specialists in the use of data launched a platform called data.org. The ultimate goal was to end extreme poverty and prevent diseases through data science.[28]

An early player in the Data4Good field is DataKind, a nonprofit organization dedicated to using data science for social good. It has chapters around the world through which volunteer data experts work with local activists on specific public inter-est projects.

One of DataKind's lead data science volunteers in Washington, DC, John McCambridge, took the lead in examin-ing the role of political influence in the allocation of Small Business Administration loans during COVID-19. Using a wide variety of data sources, John and his fellow data experts created a dashboard of loans by congressional district. They then worked with journalists to produce several important investigative arti-cles tracking loans for fraud and abuse.[29]

CONCLUSION

The evolution of smart tech has taken a route common to other technologies: a years-long slow road of development largely hid-den from public view, followed by an inflection point of fast commercialization. What would have seemed like magic just a few years ago has now become commonplace. But using smart tech and using it well are very different things. The next few chapters will focus on ways to harness smart tech and use it ethi-cally and responsibly.

ENDNOTES

1. Calestous Juma, *Innovation and Its Enemies: Why People Resist New Technologies* (Oxford, UK: Oxford University Press, 2016).
2. J. McCarthy, M. L. Minsky, N. Rochester, and C. E. Shannon, "A Proposal For The Dartmouth Summer Research Project On Artificial Intelligence" (August 31, 1955), http://www-formal.stanford.edu/jmc/history/dartmouth/dartmouth.html.
3. Clay Shirky, *Here Comes Everybody: The Power of Organizing Without Organizations* (New York: Penguin Group, 2009).

4. Jeremiah Owyang, "The Six Digital Eras" (June 3, 2019), http://web-strategist.com/blog/2019/06/03/speech-the-six-digital-eras-illuminates-a-roadmap/).

5. World Economic Forum, "These charts will change how you see the rise of AI," World Economic Forum website (December 19, 2017), https://medium.com/world-economic-forum/these-charts-will-change-how-you-see-the-rise-of-ai-99c434d9efd).

6. United States Patent and Trademark Organization, "New benchmark USPTO study finds artificial intelligence in U.S. patents rose by more than 100% since 2002" (October 27, 2020), https://www.uspto.gov/about-us/news-updates/new-benchmark-uspto-study-finds-artificial-intelligence-us-patents-rose-more.

7. Sara Brown, "What business leaders need to know about artificial intelligence" (September 16, 2019), https://mitsloan.mit.edu/ideas-made-to-matter/what-business-leaders-need-to-know-about-artificial-intelligence.

8. #AWSishow "AWS DeepLens Powered Cat Flap" (August 9, 2019), https://www.youtube.com/watch?v=ALKz1eKj4n0.

9. Mariya Yao, "Chihuahua or muffin? My search for the best computer vision API" (October 12, 2017), https://www.freecodecamp.org/news/chihuahua-or-muffin-my-search-for-the-best-computer-vision-api-cbda4d6b425d/.

10. James Vincent, "If you can identify what's in these images, you're smarter than AI: 11 researchers collect confusing images to expose the weak spots in AI vision," *The Verge* (July 19, 2019), https://www.theverge.com/2019/7/19/20700481/ai-machine-learning-vision-system-naturally-occuring-adversarial-examples.

11. Michal Wallace, Coder, "Eliza, the Rogerian Therapist" (1999), http://psych.fullerton.edu/mbirnbaum/psych101/eliza.htm.

12. Leila Toplic, "AI in the Humanitarian Sector," Nethope blog (October 6, 2020), https://nethope.org/2020/10/06/ai-in-the-humanitarian-sector/.

13. Google, "Accelerating social good with artificial intelligence: Insights from the Google AI Impact Challenge" (February 2020), https://services.google.com/fh/files/misc/accelerating_social_

good_with_artificial_intelligence_google_ai_impact_
challenge.pdf.

14. David Rolnick, Priya L. Donti, et al., "Tackling Climate Change with Machine Learning" (November 5, 2020), https://arxiv.org/pdf/1906.05433.pdf.

15. Andrew Zolli, "Planet, Paul G. Allen Philanthropies, & Leading Scientists Team Up To Map & Monitor World's Corals In Unprecedented Detail," *Planet* (June 4, 2018), http://planet.com/pulse/planet-paul-g-allen-coral-map.

16. Alexandre Lacoste, Alexandra Luccioni, Victor Schmidt, Thomas Dandres, "Quantifying the Carbon Emissions of Machine Learning," November 4, 2019, https://arxiv.org/abs/1910.09700.

17. Compute your GPU's Carbon Emissions, https://mlco2.github.io/impact/ (August 7, 2021).

18. UNHCR, Figures at a Glance, https://www.unhcr.org/en-us/figures-at-a-glance.html (July 15, 2021).

19. USA for UNHCR, "USA for UNHCR Launches Satellite Imagery and Crowdsourcing Project to Improve Refugee Camp Planning and Maintenance" (June 15, 2018), (https://www.unrefugees.org/news/usa-for-unhcr-launches-satellite-imagery-and-crowdsourcing-project-to-improve-refugee-camp-planning-and-maintenance/).

20. Aaron Tirrell, "The Rise of the HIVE: A New Era of Crowdsourced Imagery Analysis" (August 22, 2019), https://blog.maxar.com/earth-intelligence/2019/the-rise-of-the-hive-a-new-era-of-crowdsourced-imagery-analysis.

21. Microsoft, "AI for Humanitarian Action Projects" (as of August 7, 2021), https://www.microsoft.com/en-us/ai/ai-for-humanitarian-action-projects?activetab=pivot1:primaryr3.

22. OECD Policy Responses to Coronavirus (COVID-19), "Using artificial intelligence to help combat COVID-19" (April 23, 2020), https://www.oecd.org/coronavirus/policy-responses/using-artificial-intelligence-to-help-combat-covid-19-ae4c5c21/.

23. OECD Policy Responses to Coronavirus (COVID-19), "Using artificial intelligence to help combat COVID-19" (April 23, 2020),

https://www.oecd.org/coronavirus/policy-responses/using-artificial-intelligence-to-help-combat-covid-19-ae4c5c21/.

24. National Cancer Institute, "Artificial Intelligence—Opportunities in Cancer Research" (August 31, 2020), https://www.cancer.gov/research/areas/diagnosis/artificial-intelligence.

25. H. A. Haenssle, "Man against machine: diagnostic performance of a deep learning convolutional neural network for dermoscopic melanoma recognition in comparison to 58 dermatologists," *Annals of Oncology* (August 1, 2018), https://www.ncbi.nlm.nih.gov/pubmed/29846502.

26. Alexis C. Madrigal, "How a Feel-Good AI Story Went Wrong in Flint," *The Atlantic* (January, 2019), https://www.theatlantic.com/technology/archive/2019/01/how-machine-learning-found-flints-lead-pipes/578692/.

27. Jacob Abernethy, Alex Chojnacki, Arya Farahi, Eric Schwartz, and Jared Webb, "The Search for Lead Pipes in Flint, Michigan," Cornell University Library (August 17, 2018), https://arxiv.org/abs/1806.10692.

28. Jake Porway, "Charting the 'Data for Good' Landscape," Data.org website (July 14, 2021), https://www.data.org/charting-the-data-for-good-landscape.

29. DataKind.Org, "Uncovering Inequalities & Fraud in COVID-19 Stimulus Spending: National Press Foundation & DataKind DC" (February 11, 2021), https://www.datakind.org/blog/uncovering-inequalities-and-fraud-in-covid-19-stimulus-spending-national-press-foundation-datakind-d.

CHAPTER 4

Staying Human-Centered

INTRODUCTION

Cesar Chavez said, "It was never about grapes or lettuce and always about people."[1] The same holds true for smart tech. It is not about the code or the wizardry; it's about ensuring that people matter the most. Being human-centered means prioritizing the interests, strengths, and unique talents of people over the speed and wizardry of the technology. Valuing humans has never been more important as our workplaces become more and more automated.

Smart tech is a fundamentally new way of working and has the potential to do more harm than good if treating people well inside and outside isn't the top priority. This chapter explores the differences between human and machine intelligence, describes how to marry people and bots inside of organizations, and outlines steps for designing human-centered efforts to ensure smart tech is enhancing and not subjugating the needs of people.

MAN VS. MACHINE

Since the 1950s experts have been forecasting that smart tech will reach human-level intelligence in 20 years. "In other words, it's been 20 years away for 60 years," according to MIT Professor Thomas Malone.[2]

Over the past few years, Stephen Hawking, Elon Musk, Steve Wozniak, Bill Gates, and many other big names in science and technology have expressed concerns in the media about the potential for AI to be smarter than humans. There have been a number of surveys asking when this will happen and they all reach the same conclusion: we simply don't know. But we can say with absolute confidence *that right now human and machine intelligence are not equal.*[3]

In a gross oversimplification, intelligence has two components: fact-based knowledge and emotional intelligence. Smart tech is clearly gaining ground on fact-based knowledge, but it is also in the very early stages of incorporating emotional intelligence. At the heart of emotional intelligence is empathy, understanding what other people are feeling. Smart tech is not as empathetic as people yet and may never be, but it can mimic empathy through sentiment analysis.

Smart technologies are more accurate, faster, and more consistent at doing particular tasks like filling out forms. Smart technologies never get tired or need to take a lunch break or vacation. However, currently, bots are not empathetic. What they can do is *simulate* an emotional response. For instance, a customer support chatbot may be taught to apologize in a caring or helpful tone, even calling you by your name. Imitating emotions is not the same as having them or understanding them.

People have the unique ability to imagine, problem solve, anticipate, feel, and judge changing situations, which allows us to shift perspectives. Our memories, hopes, concerns, and personality also contribute to how we react to the world around us. Smart technologies simply are not capable of empathy, love, or other emotions, yet. Stuart Russell, professor of computer science at the University of California, Berkeley, writes, ". . . while AI systems may be able to mimic human empathy, they can't truly understand what empathy is like. It's a distinction that nonprofits may not understand, but it is an essential tenet of being human-centered."[4]

The gap between human and bot intelligence is reflected in the growing field of therapy chatbots. Dr. Freud in a Box and other therapy chatbots are attractive products because they are inexpensive and always available. But research has shown that bots make terrible therapists because of the limitations of smart technology to understand subtext.[5]

There are other significant challenges to therapy bots. Private companies are often not transparent about how their algorithms work, amplifying the potential for the chatbot therapist to provide bad or biased advice.

If all this was not bad enough, there is potential to weaponize private information by sharing it with marketing companies. For instance, there's Woebot. It is a chatbot therapist providing cognitive behavioral therapy through Facebook Messenger. It is not regulated or licensed as a therapist and although it has no plan to do so today, the company could choose to sell users' data to pharmaceutical companies or employers in the future.[6]

CO-BOTTING

Getting the balance right between people and smart tech is called co-botting or augmented intelligence.[7] H. James Wilson and Paul R. Daugherty have conducted research with over 1500 companies and found that significant performance improvements happen when humans and machines work together. "Through augmented intelligence, humans and AI actively enhance each other's complementary strengths: the leadership, teamwork, creativity, and social skills of the former, and the speed, scalability, and quantitative capabilities of the latter."[8]

Smart tech is an equal opportunity job disrupter and doesn't care if a job is low paying or high paying. If it involves analysis of large amounts of data, the job is going to change. Curtis Langlotz, a radiologist at Stanford, predicts, "AI won't replace radiologists, but radiologists who use AI will replace radiologists who don't."[9]

Most experts doubt AI will replace doctors any time soon because even if an algorithm is better at diagnosing a particular problem, combining it with a doctor's experience and knowledge of the patient's individual story will lead to a better treatment and outcome.

The Trevor Project provides crisis counseling to young lesbian, gay, bisexual, transgender, queer, and questioning (LGBTQ+) people. They created Riley, a chatbot to help train counselors by providing real-life simulations of conversations with potentially suicidal teens. Riley is always available for a training session with volunteers, and that helps the staff scale the number of trained counselors without adding more resources. Riley will never work on the front line directly with youth in crisis because The Trevor Project sees this role as a human-centered one.[10]

Co-botting goes beyond working with chatbots. Benefits Data Trust is a Philadelphia-based poverty reduction organization. It created a co-botting system for integrating smart tech into its efforts to help its call-in center staff assist clients to navigate and complete public benefits' application processes. The pain point they were trying to solve was the enormous amount of time and documentation it takes for clients to apply for and receive benefits. The computer system was trained on thousands of interactions between call-in staff and clients to make recommendations among dozens of possible public benefits. The system also pre-populated forms for clients, saving staff an enormous amount of time.

Ravindar Gujarl, former chief data and technology officer from the Public Benefits Trust, told us, "At the end of the day, our role as a nonprofit is to create a human connection. We won't replace our call-in staff who directly interface with our clients. Our nonprofit's work is about building relationships with our clients. They come to us in distress and we want them not to have to worry about having to collect documents or wade through a complicated application process."[11]

These examples involved careful planning to ensure that the technology augmented and didn't replace the work of staff. There is no special formula for ensuring you get the right balance between people and technology. It takes careful planning, monitoring, and continuous adjustments to ensure your organization is staying human-centered and getting the best out of both. Without this kind of care and thoughtfulness, your nonprofit could end up adding a bot like Flippy to your staff.

In March, 2018, Miso Robotics and Caliaburger, a fast-food franchise in Southern California, announced the public debut of "Flippy," the world's first autonomous robotic kitchen assistant powered by artificial intelligence. Flippy's job was to flip burger patties and remove them from the grill for its human co-workers to put the cheese on top at the right moment and add the extras, such as lettuce and sauce, before wrapping the sandwiches for customers.

The press release for the launch described how Flippy would disrupt and transform the fast-food industry by taking over the hot, greasy, and dirty task of flipping burgers. The company touted Flippy as a cost-effective and highly efficient solution that could flip 150 burgers per hour, far more than the cooks it was replacing. What the press release didn't mention was that in addition, Flippy wouldn't complain about the low pay, scanty benefits, and long hours.[12]

After two days on the job, Flippy was fired. News of Flippy, the robot cook, went viral on social media. This prompted a surge in interest and while Flippy flipped away, the human kitchen staff could not keep up with the demand. The restaurant realized it needed to spend more time on its internal systems and training people to work side-by-side with the robots.

This story shows how easy it is for an organization to choose a bot to solve a problem without engaging staff in the process and keeping the entire system human-centered.[13,14]

HUMAN-CENTERED DESIGN

COVID-19 highlighted the bad habit some organizations have of not staying human-centered during stressful times. A hospital system in Washington State welcomed donors who had given at least $10,000 to set up vaccination appointments on an "invite-only" basis. The chief executive of a high-end nursing home and assisted-living facility in West Palm Beach, Florida, invited board members and major donors to receive immunizations. These were not the only two examples of hospitals and care facilities offering donors first shot at the shots.

Mike Geiger, president of the Association of Fundraising Professionals, said in response, "The idea of hospital systems, or any charity, ignoring protocols, guidance, or restrictions—regardless of origin—and offering certain donors and board members the opportunity to 'skip the line' and receive vaccinations ahead of their scheduled time is antithetical to the values of philanthropy and ethical fundraising."[15]

While this example is not specifically about smart tech, it illustrates how easy it is for organizations to slip away from keeping clients and patients front and center. The use of smart tech makes staying human-centered even more pressing. We recommend engaging with end users through human-centered design techniques noted in the sidebar. Human-centered design focuses on developing deep empathy for end users or those who are impacted by smart tech. At the heart of this process is designing processes and services with people, not at them, through interviews, observation, and developing personas or models of end users to test processes and assumptions.

There are many excellent tools and resources for human-centered design. The essence of these processes is to:

1. Get input from key stakeholders about what issues are most important to them.

2. Outline an idea, process, or service that delineates responsibilities.

3. Test, reflect, improve.

Public Benefits Trust used this kind of process to determine what parts of their process should be automated. Ravinder said, "You can't build an algorithm that powers a public benefit system without getting feedback from the people using it."[16]

HUMAN-CENTERED DESIGN RESOURCES

There are many excellent human-centered design resources that offer step-by-step guidance for implementing a human-centered design process, which is beyond the scope of this book. Many are techniques that any nonprofit can use without hiring an expensive consultant.

If you want to quickly get up to speed, we recommend these resources for additional reading about human-centered design. Many of these organizations also offer training.

Ideo design kit: IDEO has been a thought leader in human-centered design methods. The design firm has a nonprofit spinoff (ideo.org) that focuses on methods for nonprofits and social change and includes many free practical resources and examples. In addition, IDEO has also developed specific human-centered design methods for artificial intelligence, including these cards to help understand unintended consequences of smart technologies:

- Ideo.Org Design Kit: Methods https://www.designkit.org/methods.

- AI & Ethics: Collaborative Activities for Designers https://www.ideo.com/post/ai-ethics-collaborative-activities-for-designers.

Luma Institute: The Luma system is one of the most practical, flexible, and versatile approaches to use for design thinking. It offers a playbook with simple techniques that anyone can use.

- Luma System
  https://www.luma-institute.com/about-luma/luma-system/.

Stanford Design School: In 2018, the D-School (as it is known), launched an initiative called "Radical Access," a program and resources to develop fluency in emerging technologies as a medium of design for all people. The rationale is that for any use-case of artificial intelligence to serve us, we must be involved in the design. These two techniques are especially useful to designing human-centered algorithms or mapping problems to solutions for artificial intelligence.

- I Love Algorithms
  https://dschool.stanford.edu/resources/i-love-algorithms.

- Mapping Problems to Solutions: Artificial Intelligence
  https://dschool.stanford.edu/resources/map-the-problem-space.

Participatory machine learning: Defined as the practice of using human-centered design methods to inform the design and iteration for automation projects. Google has recently published a guide that actively involves a diversity of stakeholders—technologists, UXers, policymakers, end users, and citizens—in the process of feedback for the project. The guidebook provides an overview of how human perception drives every facet of machine learning and offers up worksheets on how to get user input.

- People + AI Guidebook
  https://pair.withgoogle.com/.

Agentive design: When designing chatbots and "intelligent agents for automation," it must be grounded in human-centered design principles. The concept was developed by Christopher Noessel, an interface designer for Watson IBM. Design principles include the focus on easy setup and informative touch points. Also, when the chatbot is working, it's out of sight. When a user must engage its touch points, they require attention and consideration. Overall, well-designed chatbots and agents require lots of constant attention to manage. Effectively designing chatbots or intelligent agents requires a lot of user testing and feedback for training. The more a chatbot or intelligent agent interacts with humans, the better it learns to respond. It is different than designing other types of technology where the user is actually performing the actions versus the programming code. The metaphor often used is that it is less like designing a hammer and more like designing a butler.

- *Designing Agentive Technology: AI That Works for People* by Christopher Noessel. Published: May 2017.

CONCLUSION

The very first step that nonprofits must do when embracing smart tech is to put humans first and deeply understand how machines and people can work together. Human-centered principles and approaches are critical for the successful use of smart technologies by nonprofits as we have discussed throughout this chapter.

ENDNOTES

1. Cesar Chavez, Today's Labor Quotes, Metro Washington Council AFL-CIO (December 10, 2018), http://www.dclabor.org/home/todays-labor-quote-cesar-chavez5536620.
2. Sara Brown, "What business leaders need to know about artificial intelligence," MIT Management Sloan School (September 16, 2019), https://mitsloan.mit.edu/ideas-made-to-matter/what-business-leaders-need-to-know-about-artificial-intelligence.
3. Max Tegmark, "Benefits & Risks of Artificial Intelligence," Future of Life Institute (June 1, 2016), https://futureoflife.org/background/benefits-risks-of-artificial-intelligence/.
4. Stuart Russell, *Human Compatible: AI and the Problem of Control* (New York: Viking, 2019).
5. Aditya Nrusimha, Vaidyam Danny Linggonegoro, and John Torous, "Changes to the Psychiatric Chatbot Landscape: A Systematic Review of Conversational Agents in Serious Mental Illness" (October 16, 2020), https://journals.sagepub.com/doi/abs/10.1177/0706743720966429.
6. Karen Brown, "Something Bothering You? Tell It to Woebot," *New York Times* (June 1, 2021), https://www.nytimes.com/2021/06/01/health/artificial-intelligence-therapy-woebot.html.
7. Gary S. Vasilash, "Cobots: 14 Things You Need to Know," Gardner Business Media (October 15, 2020), https://www.gardnerweb.com/articles/cobots-14-things-you-need-to-know.

8. H. James Wilson and Paul R. Daugherty, "Collaborative Intelligence: Humans and AI Are Joining Forces," *Harvard Business Review* (July–August 2018), https://hbr.org/2018/07/collaborative-intelligence-humans-and-ai-are-joining-forces.

9. Sara Reardon, "Rise of Robot Radiologists," *Nature* (December 18, 2019), https://www.nature.com/articles/d41586-019-03847-z.

10. Abby Ohlheiser and Karen Hao, "An AI is training counselors to deal with teens in crisis," *MIT Technology Review* (February 26, 2021), https://www.technologyreview.com/2021/02/26/1020010/trevor-project-ai-suicide-hotline-training/.

11. Author interview with Ravindar Gujar (July 31, 2020).

12. Stephanie Cirigliano, "Flippy, the World's First Autonomous Robotic Kitchen Assistant, Now Cooks Burgers at CaliBurger in Pasadena, California," *Businesswire* (March 5, 2018), https://www.businesswire.com/news/home/20180305005300/en/Flippy-World%E2%80%99s-Autonomous-Robotic-Kitchen-Assistant-Cooks.

13. Scott Neuman, " 'Flippy' the Fast Food Robot (Sort Of) Mans the Grill at Caliburger," NPR (March 5, 2018), https://www.npr.org/sections/thetwo-way/2018/03/05/590884388/flippy-the-fast-food-robot-sort-of-mans-the-grill-at-caliburger.

14. Jefferson Graham, "Flippy the burger-flipping robot is on a break already," *USA Today*, https://www.usatoday.com/story/tech/talkingtech/2018/03/07/flippy-burger-flipping-robot-break-already/405580002/.

15. Eden Stiffman, "Fundraisers' Group Condemns Letting Donors and Board Members Jump the Vaccine Line," *Chronicle Of Philanthropy* (February 2, 2021), https://www.philanthropy.com/article/fundraisers-group-condemns-letting-donors-and-board-members-jump-the-vaccine-line.

16. Author interview with Ravindar Gujar (July 31, 2020).

CHAPTER 5

Data, Data, Data

INTRODUCTION

Data is the lifeblood of smart technology. Data is being generated, stored, organized, analyzed, summarized, and used to make predictions in bigger and faster ways than ever. Every organization that has a digital presence of some kind, and that is almost every organization, is generating large amounts of data. However, generating data and using it well are not the same thing.

Organizations may have a lot of data, but it is unlikely to be clean or prepped for action (even for use by an outside vendor). Or an organization may not have a plan for analyzing it. This is how you become a DRIP (Data-Rich, Information-Poor).[1,2] According to France Q. Hoang of boodle.AI, "The biggest challenge in implementing AI is getting good data. Nonprofits can use their donor and prospect lists; however, the problem with this data is that it is often messy, contains duplicates, or information is too skinny [not enough variables]." Hoang says that these flaws make it difficult to train an algorithm to be accurate.

Smart tech systems need high-quality data sets that are complete, clean (meaning the entries are correct and complete), and very, very big.

This chapter begins with an overview of how much data is being generated digitally right now, provides an introduction to data science and scientists, and outlines how your organization needs to prepare its own data and work with outside data providers. We end with some ways we hope you will explore pooling your data with other nonprofits'.

BIG DATA

Every second of every day a mind-boggling amount of data is being created, stored, shared, used, and reviewed by machines to track, analyze, and make predictions about people's behavior. We call this "big data." To do this requires "Library of Congress" amounts of data. However, even the Library of Congress is collecting "Library of Congress" amounts of data nearly every day. In the last ten years, the amount of digital items the library is storing has jumped from 10 terabytes to 74 terabytes.[3,4]

To put this in a way we can understand, a 300-page book is approximately 600 kilobytes, which means the digital collection of the Library of Congress includes roughly 123,333,333 books.[5]

These amounts pale in comparison to what is being collected by Big Tech and Big Government. For instance, the National Security Agency (NSA) collects a Library of Congress–sized amount of data *every six hours*.[6]

Here are just a few more data points for context:

- Google processes more than 3.5 billion searches a day. 1.7 MB of data was created every second by every person during 2020.

- 2.5 quintillion bytes of data are produced every day.

- In the last two years alone, 90% of the world's data has been created.[7]

The social sector has been aggregating big data as well. Table 5.1 shows commonly used data sets by sector.

To understand how data is powering smart tech, we need to begin by exploring data science.

Table 5.1   Examples of Commonly Used Data Sets

Sector	Commonly Used Data Sets
Crisis Response	Satellite images Social media
Economic Empowerment	Business transaction records Census and socioeconomic data
Education	Student and school records User data from mobile apps
Environment	Satellite data Weather data
Equality and Inclusion	Census data Specific public databases Legal cases and outcomes Survey data Glossaries
Health	Electronic health records Medical imaging Historical infectious disease outbreak records
Public Sector	Procurement data from individual counties Satellite images Unstructured text data from current requests

Source: Data from "Accelerating social good with artificial intelligence: Insights from the Google AI Impact Challenge," (February 2020), https://services.google.com/fh/files/misc/accelerating_social_good_with_artificial_intelligence_google_ai_impact_challenge.pdf.

UNDERSTANDING DATA SCIENCE

A brand-new field has been created to analyze big data. It's called data science. The people doing this work are naturally called data scientists. A data scientist has skills in computer science, statistics, and mathematics. They clean, analyze, and model data and then interpret the results into an actionable strategy for their organizations. Data scientists are analytical experts who utilize their skills in both technology and social science to find trends and manage data. They use industry knowledge, contextual understanding, and skepticism of existing assumptions to uncover solutions to problems. This is a very new profession with such huge demand that there are shortages of data scientists around the world.

Climate predictions sit at the intersection of data science and climate science. Climate informatics covers a range of topics: from improving prediction of extreme events such as hurricanes, floods, and heat waves to using large-scale models to predict the socioeconomic impacts of weather and climate.

Please don't confuse the work a data scientist does with the analysis you might do using an Excel spreadsheet. That is like comparing a bicycle with a rocket ship. Data scientists search and analyze millions of data points to make predictions or automate tasks. This is the kind of effort that was previously reserved for, say, scientists at NIH working on human genome mapping.

We appreciate that most organizations won't have a data scientist on staff. However, it is still critically important to understand what data science is and how it works in order to use smart tech well.

Here is an overview of the steps used to prepare data for use by smart tech. These are all critically important tasks to ensure that algorithms have the right, unbiased fuel to work well.

Collect: Raw data is collected from relevant sources using different methods including manual entry, automated entry, and imports from third-party databases. Nonprofits have been collecting data for years in their fundraising efforts through programs and digital communications. In addition, organizations can obtain data from the web by a process called "scrapping." For instance, likes and comments from social platforms can be "scrapped" and used.

Clean: Raw data needs to be cleaned and standardized in order to train smart tech systems. This includes simple but time-consuming processes such as fixing typos or other inaccuracies, removing or combining duplicate entries, and combining or separating different data fields. Think about the adage "Garbage in, garbage out" at this step.

Label: Labeling means consistently identifying different categories or "fields" of data points. Let's say you have two different data sets for fundraising. One has a field called "Name" with first and last name in one field. The other has two fields, "First Name" and "Last Name." The labeling procedure would be to determine which standard you want to use and changing one to fit the new standard. Labeling can be automated, but only after a person has set the standard and begun the process manually to check for accuracy.

Append: Your data is called "first-party," and commercially available data sets are called "third-party." Appending data means combining your data with third-party data. The combined data is then aggregated into a data warehouse (or data lake) for analysis.

Preprocess: It is important to have a test run of your data and the algorithm. This is to check the data's suitability for use with predictive analytics or machine learning (or other analytical methods).

Train: The preprocessed and cleaned data set(s) are used to train an algorithm to spot a pattern and make a decision. Training algorithms is done by programmers to make predictions and decisions more accurate. The data used to help algorithms practice their calculations is called "training data." No magic numbers exist for exactly how much data is needed to train systems. For instance, FaceNet, a facial recognition software system, needs 450,000 samples to begin to train its systems. Transperfect, a translation system, needs 4 million words to train its system. Improving text chats using South African language only requires 3000 training samples.[8]

Analyze: This is where the discovery happens—where all the work results in insights from the data. Algorithms might use statistical analysis, predictive analytics, and regression analysis to extract insights from the data.

Communicate: Finally, the insights are presented as reports, charts, and other data visualizations. This is a crucially important step to ensure that decision-makers can understand and use the results.

DATA PLANNING FOR YOUR ORGANIZATION

The biggest technical challenge for nonprofit organizations using smart tech is that their data isn't ready to be used.

Here are the steps for preparing your data for use in smart tech systems:

1. **Data audit.** What do we have and what shape is it in? Is our data labeled? Have duplicates been removed? Is it accurate?

2. **Stewardship preparedness.** Are staff members prepared to be good data stewards? Are we helping staff understand why data is so important, how it is collected and used, and their role in keeping it clean?

3. **Data strategy.** Do we have a plan for how to intend to use data within smart tech systems? Do we need help preparing our data? Will we need third-party data to augment what we have?

4. **Ethical stewardship.** Are our data efforts transparent with staff and clients? Are we reporting to our board on our use of internal and external data?[9,10]

We encourage you and your organization to refer to Chapter 4's "Human-Centered Design Resources" sidebar and the "Resources/Bibliography" at the end of the book for more information on preparing your data.

THIRD-PARTY DATA SETS

As mentioned earlier, third-party data may be appended to your data for use within smart tech systems. Popular third-party data sources include:

- Oracle Data Cloud
- SalesForce Marketing Cloud
- Acxiom
- Google
- Facebook
- Amazon
- Experian

- Visa

- Satellite images

- Mapping data

Third-party data may include demographics, donation, lifestyle, and consumer data.

Second-Party Data

There is still another kind of data that splits the difference between the first party and the third party; it is "second-party" data, meaning data created through collaboration with other organizations. There are three approaches to using second-party data: open data sets, data collaboratives, and crowdsourcing data.

Open Data Sets

Large open data sets are important tools for public policy and social good efforts. They are stores of data across common organizations that are available for analysis by anyone. The cost of healthcare is a perfect example of how open data sets can be used for good.

Ashley Pintos went to the emergency room at St. Joseph Medical Center in Tacoma, Washington, with a sharp pain in her stomach. She was repeatedly asked how much money she had to pay for the exam. $500? $200? $100? When Ashley responded that she had no money to pay, she was reluctantly treated and sent home with instructions to buy an over-the-counter pain medication. St. Joseph sent her a bill for $839. When she couldn't pay, the hospital referred the bill to a collection agency, which she said damaged her credit and resulted in a higher interest rate when she applied for a mortgage.

Under the Affordable Care Act, Ashley was supposed to receive a financial aid form when she first said she couldn't pay for the visit. She was not supposed to be repeatedly harangued to pay a certain amount, and she certainly wasn't supposed to be billed an enormous amount afterward. Doing so threatened St. Joseph's nonprofit status.[11]

The last part of that sentence is the key to this story. St. Joseph is a nonprofit hospital and as such is required to submit tax returns to the IRS. Because of the hard work of organizations such as Aspen Institute, the Urban Institute, and Candid, these data sets are open to the public for review and analysis. This is why we know how St. Joseph treats its low-income patients and how they're not alone in doing so. St. Joseph is part of a larger trend of nonprofit hospitals routinely trying to squeeze money out of low-income people. An analysis of the data found, ". . . 45% of nonprofit hospital organizations are routinely sending medical bills to patients whose incomes are low enough to qualify for charity care, according to a Kaiser Health News analysis of reports the nonprofits submit annually to the Internal Revenue Service. Those 1134 organizations operate 1651 hospitals."[12]

More open data sets would be enormously helpful to public policy makers to assess the efficacy of service providers.

Data Collaboratives

The amount of data and expertise needed for smart tech is beyond the capacity of most individual nonprofits. However, there is another choice beyond relying on commercial vendors. Nonprofit data collaboratives with sister organizations pool large amounts of data from organizations with a similar purpose.

The GivingTuesday Data Commons has over 100 US collaborators and 47 global data labs and is the largest philanthropic data collaboration ever built, collaborating on research and sharing findings and best practices. It collects and evaluates donation data on an ongoing basis spanning more than 10 years, as well as data about non-financial generosity behavior, to understand the patterns of when and why people give in order to predict future giving behavior.[13]

There are a huge number of variables fed into the GivingTuesday analysis including the time of the solicitation, length, and emotion, but the goal isn't just to elicit a response; it is to make people more generous in their behaviors: more generous in how much they give *and* how much information they share about the cause with other people *and* how often they come back and give again.

They use advanced analytics with a large variety of data points including topics, perspective of the speaker, and emotional content of the story. These data points are plotted against success metrics to better understand what triggers generosity.

According to Woodrow Rosenbaum, chief data officer of GivingTuesday, there is often a misconception about what it means to analyze giving data: "There is an assumption when people are looking at the transaction records, patterns of giving that they assume they are measuring donor behavior," he said. "We are equally measuring fundraiser behavior because you rarely get a donation unless you ask for one." Increasingly fundraising is mediated by technology platforms, so how these platforms are programmed to behave—when to ask, how much to ask for—will influence outcomes for individuals and organizations.

Thorn is another nonprofit creating a global data collaborative. Thorn uses smart technology to defend children from sexual abuse. Since 2016, Thorn's signature tech tool, Spotlight, has been used by law enforcement agencies across the country to spot local victims of child sex trafficking online.

Thorn's technology combines face detection and person identification, social network analysis, natural language processing, and analytics to identify child victims of sexual exploitation on the internet. Spotlight has helped law enforcement identify more than 17,000 child sex trafficking victims. On average nine children a day are identified.[14]

The design process at Thorn involves an enormous amount of stakeholder input and testing. Julie Cordua, CEO, told us that "one of Thorn's goals is to ensure the tools we develop are able to benefit the entire field of those working on child protection."[15]

The Himalayan Cataract Project's data collaborative operates on a smaller scale. The organization cures blindness around the world through simple and inexpensive cataract surgery. It is building a shared framework for how patient data is gathered, distributed, and used among ophthalmologic health organizations. This common standard not only gives health workers better insights on how to treat patients who may be served by multiple organizations but also ensures their privacy by imposing strict guidelines on how the data is used.[16]

Crowdsourcing Data

Data sets can also be crowdsourced, gathered by large numbers of people who submit data via the internet, social media, and smartphone apps. Crowdsourced data is relatively inexpensive to gather and often timely because it can be gathered in real time. However, it requires a large network of people and easy submission processes to be successful. In addition, it is important to be mindful of biases that might be introduced based on who is gathering the data.[17]

A team at the Legal Innovation and Technology Lab at Suffolk University Law School in Boston, with funding from The

Pew Charitable Trusts, built Spot, an application programming interface (API). This is software that runs in the background and feeds information to other tools and websites. For instance, this is the functionality that enables us to sign into websites using our Facebook or Google login. Spot, shorthand for legal issue spotter, crowdsources the data that lies beneath a chatbot or a smart form on a legal services website. It can also help fill out forms for client intake.[18]

Spot has descriptions of legal issues created by real people to describe common civil legal issues such as eviction, foreclosure, bankruptcy, divorce, and others. It directs people to the right help. Spot's founder, David A. Colarusso, says, "People don't use the same language as an attorney to describe legal problems. No one does a search for 'constructive eviction.' They say, 'My landlord is being a jerk.' " The point is that constructive eviction, doesn't actually have to do with an eviction; it has to do with a landlord being a jerk by not doing their job. So there's almost no way a layperson would use the term properly, and that's the point. Spot attempts to translate a layperson's usage (e.g., "my landlord's being a jerk because he won't fix the heat") to labels like constructive eviction.[19]

Hundreds of volunteers on a legal advice forum on Reddit added labels to the data. However, this added the possibility of bias because Reddit's site is overwhelmingly made of white, male professionals. To mitigate the potential for bias, Spot also appended data from legal aid nonprofits about how their clients describe legal issues.

CONCLUSION

In this chapter, we offered a crash course in understanding data and data science. And while you don't necessarily need to know how to code an algorithm or label a data set, you do need to know the process for preparing data to use with smart tech. There is still one very important topic you need to dive into first before getting ready to use smart tech, and that is ethical and responsible use, which we discuss in the next chapter.

ENDNOTES

1. Robert H. Waterman Jr. and Tom Peters, *In Search of Excellence* (New York: HarperCollins, 1983).
2. NationSwell Data for Good Insight Report, March 2021, https://nationswell.com/wp-content/uploads/2021/03/NationSwell-BIBB-Data-for-Good-Insights-Report-2020.pdf.
3. Contel Bradford, "Big Data Storage and Preservation at the Library of Congress," Storage Craft blog, July 25 (no year), https://blog.storagecraft.com/big-data-storage-library-congress/.
4. "Terabytes and Kilobytes Converter," The Calculator Site as of August 8, 2021, https://www.thecalculatorsite.com/conversions/datastorage/terabytes-kilobytes.php.
5. Anonymous et al., "How many books does 8GB hold?" Best Buy website as of August 8, 2021, https://www.bestbuy.com/site/questions/amazon-fire-hd-7-8gb-black/8932052/question/c65444fe-aa67-3d6d-933e-22703775bc7c).
6. Husain Sumra, "The NSA Collects a Library of Congress Worth of Data Every Six Hours," Gizmodo (May 10, 2011), https://gizmodo.com/the-nsa-collects-a-library-of-congress-worth-of-data-ev-5800512.
7. Jacquelyn Bulao, "How Much Data Is Created Every Day in 2021?" (August 6, 2021), https://techjury.net/blog/how-much-data-is-created-every-day/#gref.
8. Telus International, "How much AI training data do you need?" (January 1, 2021), https://lionbridge.ai/articles/how-much-ai-training-data-do-you-need/.
9. Nethope, "The Nonprofit Data Journey" (June 17, 2021), https://nethope.org/2021/06/17/the-nonprofit-data-journey/.

10. Rachel Rank, "How to Build a Data Culture" (February 3, 2020), https://www.threesixtygiving.org/2020/02/03/how-to-build-a-data-culture/).

11. Jordan Rau, "Free or Discounted Care Is Available at Some Hospitals But They Don't Make It Easy," October 11, 2019, https://www.washingtonpost.com/business/economy/free-or-discounted-care-is-available-at-some-hospitals-but-they-dont-make-it-easy/2019/10/10/8ad4c540-e92a-11e9-9c6d-436a0df4f31d_story.html.

12. Jordan Raum, Kaiser Family Foundation, "Patients Eligible for Charity Care Instead Get Big Bills," October 11, 2019 , https://khn.org/news/patients-eligible-for-charity-care-instead-get-big-bills/.

13. Author interview with Woodrow Rosenbaum, June 1, 2021.

14. Thorn, "Our Work Is Guided by Three Principles" (accessed on August 24, 2021) (https://www.thorn.org/our-work-to-stop-child-sexual-exploitation/).

15. Author interview with Julie Cordua, April 1, 2021.

16. Cure Blindness, "The Gift of Sight" (accessed on August 24, 2021), https://www.cureblindness.org/.

17. The World Bank Wiki, Crowdsourced Data, (accessed on August 24, 2021), https://dimewiki.worldbank.org/Crowd-sourced_Data.

18. The Legal Innovation & Technology Lab's Spot API, "Spot's Training Data" (accessed on August 24, 2021), https://spot.suffolklitlab.org/data/.

19. Author interview with David A. Colarusso on June 2, 2021.

CHAPTER 6

Ethical and Responsible Use

INTRODUCTION

In a 2017 survey 55% of US human resource managers said AI would be a regular part of their work within five years. There was no corresponding question about how these managers would work to make sure their smart tech is actively anti-biased in engaging and empowering all people fairly equally.[1] This fast commercialization of smart tech products is outpacing our collective understanding of their ethical and responsible usage. As Shalini Kantayya, the director of Coded Bias, said to us, "We could roll back fifty years in civil rights advances if we blindly trust the algorithms."[2]

Spiderman's motto, "With great power comes great responsibility," applies to users of smart tech.[3] Whether you are an executive, team member, consultant, or customer, using smart tech ethically is one of your essential responsibilities.

Machines making decisions for people in ways that are largely invisible creates opportunities for intentional and unintentional misuse that need to be carefully watched and mitigated. For instance, bankruptcy claims gathered from the web by financial companies can then be used to offer predatory deals.

In this chapter, we will examine three critically important areas: responsible use, bias, and privacy. We will discuss real-life circumstances where these concerns have created ethical dilemmas. Finally, we will provide guidance for your organization to ensure that smart tech does far more good than harm in your organization and in the world.

RESPONSIBLE USE

The awesome power of smart tech creates a responsibility for decision makers to reduce potential harm to people and organizations and use the technology well. The cyber-security field uses the term "threat modeling" to envision what could go wrong in a project: what data could be compromised, what system could be hacked, and what user could be harmed.[4] It is a risk-based planning approach to ensure the safe and secure use of smart tech. We recommend a similar kind of process that continues through the life of a smart tech effort.

Allen Gunn ("Gunner") is the executive director of Aspiration, a nonprofit dedicated to the ethical and responsible use of tech for good and an expert on risk management for digital technologies. He told us, "We have to imagine the negative impact of automated decision making." He continued, ". . . nonprofits need to discuss and identify worst-case scenarios." Gunn also advises organizations to challenge every pain point and benefit to make sure smart tech is the right solution. He advised end users to be particularly careful about collecting and storing user data.[5]

It is responsible to think carefully, strategically, and slowly about the use of smart tech and walk through whether smart tech is creating problems, how it is doing so, and how they can be mitigated. It is irresponsible to rush decision-making without taking into account the ramifications of automating decisions and the impact on constituents inside and outside of an organization.

Table 6.1 shows some instances where nonprofits need to think about the responsible use of smart tech.[6]

Let's take one issue: the risk of your data system being hacked. Here are steps you can take to mitigate this risk:

- Make a list of organizations, government entities, or other groups that might use these assets for good or bad. What might they use the data for?

- Identify ways that you would change what data you are collecting or how it is used or stored to mitigate this risk. List what data should be excluded, limited, or specifically

Table 6.1   Some Potential Risks of Smart Tech

Who Is Affected	Risks
Individuals/End Users (Staff, Clients, or Donors)	Clients in crisis are served late or not at all. People are not treated equitably. We don't protect people's data privacy. Clients are denied benefits or not hired for a job due to a biased algorithm or data set.
Organizations	Automated financial reports are flawed because of faulty predictive algorithms. Staff job performance reviews are unfair. Screening of resumes is biased. Information about clients is disclosed inappropriately. Clients can't reach staff. Risks aren't mitigated, and the public loses trust in the organization, damaging its reputation.

protected. Ask how you could accomplish this without jeopardizing the beneficial intent of your design. For example, would it be easy to anonymize names to make it more difficult to cross-reference with other sources?

- Test your system with these limitations, and see if you can achieve your desired result.[7]

ROOTING OUT EMBEDDED BIAS

Bias means systematically favoring one group over another. The big cultural areas of bias that society typically focuses on include gender, race, LGBTQ+, ableism, ageism, religion, class, education, and nationality, although many other areas of bias exist as well. Bias built into smart tech is very difficult to mitigate because programmers may not be aware that they are skewing systems, and the effect of bias is difficult to see unless one specifically tests for it. That's why we call it "embedded bias." Let's examine an extreme example of the harm embedded bias can cause.

Nijeer Parks was arrested at his house on February 13, 2019. He was charged with shoplifting candy and trying to hit a police officer with a car at a Hampton Inn in Woodbridge, New Jersey. The police identified Nijeer using facial recognition software. This kind of product is used by law enforcement agencies to match a photo from a crime scene with one in a database of millions of images. Unfortunately, law enforcement departments are often using grainy, unlit images from crime scenes. In addition, the data used to train these systems often underrepresents communities of color, which then makes it harder to distinguish between people of color.

We will probably never know precisely why the software the police used mistakenly identified Nijeer as the prime suspect in this case. We do know that Nijeer had no connection to the crime and could prove he was 30 miles away at the time of the incident. It took nine months for the case to be dismissed, Nijeer paid $5000 in legal fees, and the arrest stands in the public record, available for, say, a future employer. Perhaps worst of all, the police refused to admit the facial recognition software was biased and continued to use it as part of their criminal investigations.[8,9]

Biases created by smart tech don't always show up in such dramatic ways. For instance, Amazon has an almost insatiable need for computer engineers. The company did what it does best and built an algorithm to solve the problem. After all, they already had two of the main ingredients: technical expertise and a huge historic dataset of successful Amazon engineers. Basically, they built a smart tech system to go out and get more of what they already had. And by that standard it was wildly successful—if what you wanted was a company full of men. The system favored candidates who described themselves using verbs like "executed" and "captured," which more commonly appeared on male engineers' resumes. The result was that Amazon built an AI system that replicated its long history of gender bias.[10]

An executive using smart tech to, say, screen resumes, won't necessarily know who *didn't* get past the algorithmic gatekeeper, although we know it is likely that those who are screened out are Black and Brown people.

In transitive terms: bias is embedded in smart tech code, smart tech is embedded within organizations, and therefore organizations using biased smart tech are biased and discriminatory. Nonprofit organizations need to become *actively anti-biased* in their choice and implementation of smart tech. This needs to become a fundamental part of every organization's diversity and inclusion work.

Efforts to fight embedded bias begin with knowledge. Decision makers need to understand what smart tech is and how and why embedded bias is affecting their organization's activities and reputation.

At its core, embedded bias reflects the demographics of programmers who continue to be overwhelmingly white and male. The share of women in computing today is 26%—lower than it was in 1960.[11] Racial diversity is negligible at the largest tech firms. In the US, 4.5% of Microsoft's employees are Black and 6.3% are Hispanic/Latinx.[12]

These examples show how easy it is for developers to use smart tech to intensify rather than remediate bias and discrimination. Embedded bias is insidious; it sneaks up on people in invisible and unexpected ways. For instance, neither the person applying for a job (or health insurance or food assistance) *nor* generally the person helping them knows the system is biased until it's too late. Sadly, it is nearly impossible for this not to happen. The only thing we can do is be aware of the probability of bias built into code and test systems early and often to try to reduce the bias. As Jill Finlayson of UC Berkeley says, "You cannot correct bias, you can only mitigate it."[13]

Embedded bias sneaks into smart tech in three ways:

- The data sets used to train the systems have historic bias built into them. Calestous Juma wrote, "History does not repeat itself, but its echoes can be heard all around us."[14] Those echoes are our new computer code. The Amazon example proved how easy a trap this is to fall into.

- The model itself is biased. This is particularly true when proxy questions are used to answer a question. Sarah Wysocki, a public school teacher in Washington, DC, was fired because an automated performance system determined she had poor results. It turned out that the model was fundamentally flawed, using poor proxies for teacher performance and faulty data sets.[15] This is more likely to happen when end users are not involved in the development of code and products.

- The system is used in ways it wasn't intended. This was a large part of the problem with the VI-SPDAT that we discussed in Chapter 1, "Becoming a Smart Nonprofit." It was intended as a triage tool but was generally used as an overall assessment instrument.

The responsibility to check for embedded bias doesn't just rest on tech companies. End users also have a responsibility to test for bias. For years, users of the VI-SPDAT kept using it even though many of them had a nagging feeling that something was wrong with the results. These organizations let their clients down by not building into their efforts systematic ways of checking their own results for bias. We discuss specific ways for checking your systems for bias at the end of this chapter. Before doing that, we need to explore who owns all of the data swimming around in smart tech systems.

DIGITAL PRIVACY

The right to personal privacy is a relatively new legal concept. Samuel Warren and Louis Brandeis, prior to becoming Supreme Court Justices, wrote a seminal paper in 1890 on the legal foundation for a person's right to hold certain parts of their life private from the government. They described a common law assumption that every person had the right to be free from the interference of corporations or governments. In particular, they were concerned with a new kind of "yellow" journalism that had "invaded sacred precincts of private and domestic life." The need for and right to privacy, they felt, was a triumph of civilization and modernity, not a fault of it.[16] Prior to Brandeis's seminal work in this area there was no legal protection for a person's thoughts, ideas, opinions, and personal information. Brandeis termed the right to personal privacy as the "right to be left alone." It is the presumption of self-determination and the right of each person to decide what information and aspects of their lives will be private and what will be public.[17]

Not coincidentally, the 1890s were also a moment of incredible technological advancements including inexpensive, portable cameras, sound recording devices, and the continuing growth of the telegraph, all of which related to journalism, how it was used, and the effect it might have on personal privacy.[18]

Several seminal Supreme Court rulings addressed privacy as well, largely siding with individuals on when, where, and how their thoughts, likenesses, and private conversations could be recorded and shared. One was *Griswold v. Connecticut* in 1965, wherein the Supreme Court ruled that the state banning the use of birth control violated the right to marital privacy.[19] Another ruling addressed bugging public spaces in *Katz. v. United States* in 1967.

The explosion of digital tech and the internet in the 1990s changed privacy in a way no one had ever predicted. Corporations didn't need to take or steal our data; we voluntarily gave it to them, all of it. We incessantly and enthusiastically fed them our personal information, thoughts, feelings, connections, and photos online on platforms that are legally protected from liability. We signed their overly complicated user agreements, uploaded, commented, and liked everything that they then used to make money. It continues to be a brilliant, diabolical invasion of privacy.

In 2009, it was reported that Google made individual search histories available to law enforcement agencies without users' permission. Rather than being contrite, Google Chairperson Eric Schmidt cavalierly said, "If you have something that you don't want anyone to know, maybe you shouldn't be doing it in the first place, but if you really need that kind of privacy, the reality is that search engines including Google do retain this information for some time."[20] Schmidt also noted that there was potential for the information to be made available to law enforcement. The argument that there is nothing to hide if you haven't done anything wrong is the exact opposite of Brandeis's position on privacy.

An overwhelming number of people are unhappy about the state of data privacy. This includes some tech titans like Apple CEO Tim Cook. He said, "Technology does not need vast troves of personal data stitched together across dozens of websites and apps in order to succeed. Advertising existed and thrived for decades without it, and we're here today because the path of least resistance is rarely the path of wisdom."[21]

There are significant personal benefits of using digital tech to keep up with family and friends, share news and photos, raise awareness of causes, and for a few hardworking people, making money as influencers. In our collective cost/benefit analysis of convenience versus keeping our information private, we chose convenience. For many people, buying a computer online on Tuesday and having it show up on your doorstep on Wednesday outweighs concerns about how the computer company will use your information. It even outweighs the annoyance of having advertisements for computer accessories show up in your online feeds for months. However, our slide into privacy equivocation has created two new kinds of capitalism that are essential tools for bad actors: surveillance capitalism and reputation capital.

Surveillance Capitalism

Tracking people's thoughts, conversations, movements, and photos and videos creates enormous stores of data about the habits, activities, and proclivities of individuals that can be used to track people online and on land. This industry is called surveillance capitalism.[22]

Of course, surveillance isn't a new idea or activity; it has a long and sinister history in the United States.

In eighteenth century New York, Black people were required to carry lanterns at light to be publicly visible to other citizens and particularly to the police. These "lantern laws" persisted for decades and were replaced by police efforts to surveil low-income communities of color with overhead helicopters and flood lights throughout the night. The latest iteration of racial surveillance is facial recognition software. In 2016, the city of Detroit installed high-definition cameras throughout the city. The data collected from the cameras is streamed directly to the police departments and fed into facial recognition software with data from driver's licenses, crime databases, and other state information. Information about almost every Michigan resident is somewhere within this system. However, the use of the data against Michiganders isn't equally distributed because the cameras are disproportionately located in low-income neighborhoods, disproportionately affecting Black, Brown, and poor White neighborhoods.[23]

The everyday surveillance of citizens is going to increase exponentially as public and private tracking systems continue to grow unchecked.

Reputation Capital

A new form of capital created by big data is reputation capital. In 2014, the Chinese government introduced a national system for gauging the reputation of citizens in order to create a society wherein "keeping trust is glorious and breaking trust is disgraceful."[24]

The exact measures are not made public but include indicators such as bad driving, smoking in non-smoking zones, buying too many video games, and posting fake news online, specifically about terrorist attacks or airport security.

It has had an uneven rollout with local systems varying in their measures and applications. But the overall idea is that the Chinese government will measure the good and bad behavior of its citizens and use scoring to block access to certain services: "One city, Rongcheng, gives all residents 1,000 points to start. Authorities make deductions for bad behaviour like traffic violations, and add points for good behaviour such as donating to charity."[25,26]

The scores can then be used to block or provide access to loans or housing or even riding on trains.

Spiraling Out of Control

Here's what can happen when our personal privacy is of no concern to the code makers:

Luda was an AI chatbot created in 2021 by ScatterLab, a Korean computer company. ScatterLab runs "Science of Love," an app that provides dating advice based on analysis of text exchanges.[27] The app has been downloaded over 2.7 million times in South Korea and Japan. Why not use the 10 billion conversations from the app, the company thought, to build a simulated 20-year-old female college student for conversations with lovelorn people to have even more conversations about love? And let's put this simulation on Facebook Messenger, one of the most insecure platforms on the entire web. And as a bonus, we're going to download even more data from the open data platform GitHub without asking users for permission to use their data. What could go wrong?

Luda was quickly trained to use hate speech fed by trolls. But there was another problem Luda displayed. It integrated very personal information into conversations with users, names, nicknames, home addresses, and even bank account information it had gleaned from Science of Love app data and data it downloaded from GitHub.[28]

In her book *How We Give Now*, Lucy Bernholz describes the variety of ways individual data is being captured, catalogued, and used by corporations and nonprofits. These include donations, images (like photos of flowers for crowdsourced databases), liking and sharing social media posts, and signing petitions. These small transactions are creating enormous databases of information about our behavior, interests, political persuasions, locations, social networks, and more.[29]

It would be a fool's errand to believe we will return to an early twentieth-century notion of privacy. There is simply too much data being produced and processed every second for legitimate and illegitimate purposes to go back to pre-digital norms of privacy. Bernholz writes, "The public pendulum of awareness seems to have swung from 'I don't understand' to 'I don't care' to 'I don't know what to do about it,' the idea that a person could be in charge of how their own data are used is still new."[30]

However, we can insist on flipping the tables and requiring companies to come to us and ask for permission for time-limited, one-time use of it for a specific purpose—the right to own our personal data. There have been some organizations such as the ACLU and the Center for the Humane Use of Technology discussing this, but most nonprofits have been largely absent from this discussion. That was a choice—and a shame—for what is shaping up to be the next fight for civil liberties.

This won't be an easy fight to win. Big Tech is virulently opposed to it, which may be the best reason to fight for it. The nonprofit sector is perfectly positioned to become models for prioritizing the rights of our constituents, donors, volunteers, and clients, over the desire to use their data for fundraising and marketing. Consider that nonprofits follow commercial norms for requiring constituents to opt out of data systems rather than opt in. Meaning, we hold their data captive, for as long as we like, unless they specifically ask to get out. We will discuss ways to prioritize individual data rights next.

CREATING ETHICAL STANDARDS

The nonprofit sector should voluntarily take the lead and hold itself to the highest ethical standards for smart tech. This may seem counterintuitive for a sector known for lagging technologically, but doing so aligns with our fundamental purpose of making the world a healthier, safer, cleaner, greener, and more vibrant and loving place. Our sector makes up over 25% of the GDP and includes religious organizations, universities, and nonprofit healthcare providers. Perhaps most importantly, we have no commercial stake in the data industries.[31]

There are a number of outstanding nonprofit organizations providing guidance on the ethical use of smart tech. They include NetHope, American Council for Technology-Industry Advisory Council (ACT-IAC), and Berkeley Haas Business School. We encourage every organization to institute their own ethical standards for the use of smart tech, discuss these issues regularly and widely with stakeholders, and stay current in this very quickly developing field.

We recommend beginning by creating an outside ethics review board. The software company Axon did, and it proved exceptionally helpful in their efforts.

Axon develops facial recognition software. They created an outside ethics board that operates independently of the organization and has, as its members, experts in the fields of AI, computer science, privacy, law enforcement, civil liberties, and public policy. The board was asked to weigh in on the use of facial recognition software for policing. After a year of meetings it reported "that face recognition technology is not yet reliable enough to justify its use on body-worn cameras," and expressed particular concern regarding "evidence of unequal and unreliable performance across races, ethnicities, genders and other identity groups."[32] As a result of the investigation, the board asked Axon to stop the development of facial recognition products, including body-worn cameras. Axon agreed to this and other recommendations of the board.

We strongly encourage every organization, regardless of size or purpose, to create, or have access to, an ethical review board. This independent body will review cases and provide feedback on potential biases or ethical problems with AI systems. We realize that smaller organizations may not have the wherewithal to create their own board; however, this is where regional associations or membership associations can be very helpful in creating boards to serve multiple organizations. The most immediate area requiring organizational attention is transparency.

As we've mentioned before, one of the most challenging aspects of smart tech for end users is that it is mostly invisible. It is humming along in the background largely unseen like a refrigerator. But out of sight shouldn't mean out of mind. It isn't easy to see, and it certainly won't be easy to get commercial vendors to open up their black boxes, but that doesn't mean we shouldn't try. Some transparency considerations include:

- *External Stakeholders:* Are we making it clear to outside people when they are interacting with bots (e.g., online chatbots)?

- *Vendors:* Are we asking vendors where their data sets come from, what assumptions they used to develop their algorithms, and whether they share our data with third parties?

- *Internal Stakeholders:* Are we communicating with staff members where and how we're using AI to, say, assess job performance or any other ways bots are affecting their jobs and, potentially, their compensation?

SMART TECH AND GOVERNANCE

Governing boards bear the ultimate responsibility for ensuring that organizations are operating in ethical, healthy, and effective ways. Smart tech poses a particular challenge for boards because they are, necessarily, removed from the day-to-day work and may not have programmatic or technical expertise. The bigger challenge for boards is that beyond exercising their fiduciary responsibility by reviewing financial statements and budgets and fundraising support, boards are often at a loss of exactly what they should spend their time doing. This often results in being too far removed from the work or too closely involved. The ethical responsibilities of using smart tech offer a reset for boards.

Smart tech offers opportunities to recalibrate expectations and measures that have been the norms for decades. For instance, in Chapter 9, "Fundraising," we will explore the need for organizations to reset their fundraising performance around a new set of measures that focus on donor retention rather than just acquisition. Regarding smart tech writ large, here are the particular areas that need and deserve attention from governing boards:

- How well are we balancing the human/tech intersection? Are clients and other constituents able to easily access people within our organization? Do we still feel like an organization run and staffed by people?

- Are we living our values when it comes to the use of data? Are we transparent about our policies? Do we default to opt in rather than opt out? Are we scrutinizing third-party data sources?

- Are we being actively anti-biased in our use of smart tech? Are we doing our best to mitigate racial and gender biases? Are we monitoring for bias in the use of smart tech by comparing the people screened in from those who are screened out of our systems?

Individual data rights have their roots in the 1950 European Convention on Human Rights[33] which states, "Everyone has the right to respect for his private and family life, his home, and his correspondence." From this basis, the European Union built a set of laws to protect consumer's data called the General Data Protection Regulation (GDPR). Any company or organization doing business with members of the European Union needs to comply with these rules.

The essence of these rules is putting consumers in charge of when, what, and for how long their data can be used by companies. The purpose for data collection needs to be made clear in simple, understandable language and be time limited. The aim should be to collect the least amount of data, use it for a single purpose, and ensure it isn't used by anyone else. Included in these rights is the "right to be forgotten."[34] This has a similar feel to Louis Brandeis's right to be left alone. It is the notion that consumers have the right to ask companies to completely erase their data. Companies do not currently offer this right in the US. Instead, when a person says, "Unsubscribe from a mailing list," the company still keeps data about that person; it just doesn't email them spam. This is data they can still sell to another company or use for other marketing purposes.

GDPR laws have some serious bite, too. There are two tiers of penalties, which max out at €20 million or 4% of global revenue (whichever is higher), plus data subjects have the right to seek compensation for damages. This includes even nonprofits. Eleven nonprofits in the United Kingdom were fined for data breaches in 2017, including the UK Cancer Society and Guide Dogs for the Blind.[35] In July 2021, Mermaids, a British charity that provides support to gender-diverse children, young people, and their families, was fined £25,000 for failing to keep its users' data secure.[36]

There is a very different kind of future possible for both organizations and individuals if we rethink the default settings of data privacy. Kevin Scott asks, "What if the law mandated that to do business with the government, every provider of medical services, on behalf of patients, had to securely and digitally provide a record of the services rendered in a standard format into a medical record locker controlled by the patient, perhaps implemented using blockchain?"[37]

Building on the framework of the GDPR, we propose the following rights for outside constituents:

- Clear, understandable statement of what data is being collected and why.
- Right to be forgotten.

- Time-limited storage of personal data.

- Assurance that constituent data will never be used as part of discriminatory systems.

CONCLUSION

As outlined in this chapter, there are a lot of decisions to be made in order to use smart tech well. There are also important mistakes to avoid. We will save you and your organization an enormous amount of time and pain by sharing this: it is important *not* to wait for something bad to happen before looking for warning signs of potential harm. As we've seen throughout this book, it is very difficult to undo the harms of smart tech once it is implemented. Do your homework, think through the process carefully, take your time, and do your best to reduce potential harm: "If you understand where risks may be lurking, ill-understood, or simply unidentified, you have a better chance of catching them before they catch up with you."[38]

ENDNOTES

1. HRDrive, "More Than Half of HR Managers Say Artificial Intelligence Will Become a Regular Part of HR in Next 5 Years" (May 18, 2017), https://www.hrdive.com/press-release/20170518-more-than-half-of-hr-managers-say-artificial-intelligence-will-become-a-reg/.

2. Author interview with Shalini Kantayya on April 29, 2021.

3. Wikipedia, "With Great Power Comes Responsibility" (August 25, 2021), https://en.wikipedia.org/wiki/With_great_power_comes_great_responsibility.

4. Wikipedia, "Threat Model" (August 25, 2021), https://en.wikipedia.org/wiki/Threat_model.

5. Author interview with Allen Gunn on July 19, 2021.

6. Benjamin Cheatham, Kia Javanmardian, and Hamid Samandari, *McKinsey Quarterly*, "Confronting the Risks of Artificial Intelligence" (April 26, 2019), https://www.mckinsey.com/ business-functions/mckinsey-analytics/our-insights/confronting-the-risks-of-artificial-intelligence.

7. Babar Bhatti, "7 Types of AI Risk and How to Mitigate their Impact" (September 12, 2020), https://towardsdatascience.com/7-types-of-ai-risk-and-how-to-mitigate-their-impact-36c086bfd732.

8. Kashmir Hill, "Another Arrest, and Jail Time, Due to a Bad Facial Recognition Match," *New York Times* (January 6, 2021), https://www.nytimes.com/2020/12/29/technology/facial-recognition-misidentify-jail.html.

9. Alex Najibi, "Racial Discrimination in Face Recognition Technology," Harvard University Graduate School of Arts & Sciences (October 24, 2020), https://sitn.hms.harvard.edu/ flash/2020/racial-discrimination-in-face-recognition-technology/.

10. "Amazon ditched AI recruiting tool that favored men for technical jobs," *The Guardian* (October 10, 2018), https://www.theguardian. com/technology/2018/oct/10/amazon-hiring-ai-gender-bias-recruiting-engine.

11. Erik Sherman, "Report: Disturbing drop in women in computing field," *Fortune* (March 26, 2015), https://fortune.com/2015/03/26/ report-the-number-of-women-entering-computing-took-a-nosedive/.

12. Dina Bass, "Microsoft Makes Small Strides in Hiring Women and Minorities," *Bloomberg Law* (November 12, 2019), https://news. bloomberglaw.com/esg/microsoft-makes-small-strides-in-hiring-women-and-minorities.

13. Author interview with Jill Finlayson on June 25, 2021.

14. Calestous Juma, *Innovation and its Enemies: Why People Resist New Technologies* (Oxford: Oxford University Press, 2016).

15. Cathy O'Neil, *Weapons of Math Destruction: How Big Data Increases Inequality and Threatens Democracy* (New York: Penguin Random House, 2016).

16. Sarah E. Igo, *The Known Citizen: A History of Privacy in Modern America* (Cambridge: Harvard University Press, 2018).

17. Dorothy J. Glancy, "The Invention of the Right to Privacy," *Arizona Law Review*, Volume 21, 1979.

18. Dorothy J. Glancy, "The Invention of the Right to Privacy," *Arizona Law Review*, Volume 21, 1979.

19. Sarah E. Igo, *The Known Citizen: A History of Privacy in Modern America* (Cambridge: Harvard University Press, 2018).

20. Jared Newman, "Google's Schmidt Roasted for Privacy Comments," *PCWorld*, December 11, 2009, https://www.pcworld. com/article/184446/googles_schmidt_roasted_for_privacy_com- ments.html#:~:text=%22If%20you%20have%20something%20 that, all%20subject%20in%20the%20United.

21. Justin Bariso, "Tim Cook May Have Just Ended Facebook," *Inc.*, January 30, 2021, https://www.inc.com/justin-bariso/tim-cook- may-have-just-ended-facebook.html?fbclid=IwAR140K7i98xom ELt5drp7Clx_zI_hC5-XAyFJ8ANpfBNzSxhWvLJBhyW3Xk.

22. Shoshana Zuboff, "Big Other: Surveillance Capitalism and the Prospects of an Information Civilization," *SAGE* (March 1, 2015), https://journals.sagepub.com/doi/10.1057/jit.2015.5.

23. Claudia Garcia-Rojas, "The Surveillance of Blackness: From the Trans-Atlantic Slave Trade to Contemporary Surveillance Technologies," *Truthout*, March 3, 2016, https://truthout.org/ articles/the-surveillance-of-blackness-from-the-slave-trade-to- the-police/.

24. Alexandra Ma and Katie Canales, "China's 'social credit' system ranks citizens and punishes them with throttled internet speeds and flight bans if the Communist Party deems them untrustwor- thy," *Insider* (May 9, 2021), https://www.businessinsider.com/ china-social-credit-system-punishments-and-rewards-explained- 2018-4.

25. Nicole Kobie, "The complicated truth about China's social credit system," *Wired* (July 6, 2019), https://www.wired.co.uk/article/ china-social-credit-system-explained).

26. Ed Jefferson, "No, China isn't Black Mirror—social credit scores are more complex and sinister than that," *New Statesmen* (April 27, 2018), https://www.newstatesman.com/world/asia/2018/04/no-china-isn-t-black-mirror-social-credit-scores-are-more-complex-and-sinister.

27. Dongwoo Kim, "Chatbot Gone Awry Starts Conversations About AI Ethics in South Korea," *The Diplomat* (January 16, 2021), https://thediplomat.com/2021/01/chatbot-gone-awry-starts-conversations-about-ai-ethics-in-south-korea/.

28. Heeso Jang, "A South Korean Chatbot Shows Just How Sloppy Tech Companies Can Be With User Data," *Slate*, April 2, 2021, https://slate.com/technology/2021/04/scatterlab-lee-luda-chatbot-kakaotalk-ai-privacy.html).

29. Lucy Bernholz, *How We Give Now*, review copy shared with authors, page 55.

30. Lucy Bernholz, *How We Give Now*, review copy shared with authors, page 129.

31. NCCS Project Team, Nonprofit Sector Brief, Urban Institute (June, 2020), https://nccs.urban.org/publication/nonprofit-sector-brief-2019#top.

32. Axon AI Ethics Board, First Report of the Axon AI Ethics Board: Face Recognition, 2019, https://www.policingproject.org/axon-fr.

33. European Convention on Human Rights, November, 1998, https://www.echr.coe.int/Documents/Convention_ENG.pdf.

34. Right to Be Forgotten, Wikipedia (August 25, 2021), https://en.wikipedia.org/wiki/Right_to_be_forgotten.

35. Hugh Radojev, "ICO fines 11 major charities for data protection breaches" (April 5, 2017), https://www.civilsociety.co.uk/news/ico-fines-11-charities-for-breaches-of-data-protection.html.

36. Camilla Elliot, "£25,000 ICO fine is no drop in the ocean for Mermaids" (July 27, 2021), https://www.lexology.com/library/detail.aspx?g=9a17855a-4fd8-4ce2-8bc6-bedbe9b7c7a9.

37. Kevin Scott, Reprogramming The American Dream: From Rural America to Silicon Valley—Making AI Serve Us (New York: Harper Collins, 2020).

38. Benjamin Cheatham, Kia Javanmardian, and Hamid Samandari, "Confronting the Risks of Artificial Intelligence," *McKinsey Quarterly* (April 26, 2019), https://www.mckinsey.com/business-functions/mckinsey-analytics/our-insights/confronting-the-risks-of-artificial-intelligence.

PART II

THE SMART NONPROFIT USE-CASE EXAMPLES AND MANAGEMENT

CHAPTER 7

Ready, Set, Go

INTRODUCTION

Leila Toplic, head of Emerging Technologies Initiative at NetHope, emphasizes the importance of being intentional in developing adequate expertise to guide responsible design and use of AI/ML. She says, "The nonprofit sector has a responsibility to the people and the communities they support to evaluate suitability of artificial intelligence for the problems they face and to know how to guide impactful, sustainable, and ethical development and use of AI systems in humanitarian contexts."[1]

This chapter outlines a process for honing in on a specific use of smart tech, choosing your partners and tools well, and creating a thoughtful implementation process that ensures that far more good than harm will happen. It is vital that you and your organization be proactive in thinking through the specific use of smart tech, consider the benefits and potential for harm, and stay human-centered at every step.

We recommend an implementation process that includes the steps and activities shown in Table 7.1.

In this chapter, we'll explore each of these three steps.

Table 7.1   Ready, Set, Go

Ready	• Create a smart tech team of stakeholders to advise on a clear problem statement and other activities.
	• Define a strategic, mission-driven purpose by identifying an important pain point or problem to be solved.
	• Involve end users through interviews or observations to define the problem from their point of view.
	• Create a use case and user journey map to ensure a human-centered process.
	• Imagine any unintended consequences that may result from using smart tech.
Set	• Identify potential tools, vendors, and technical consultants.
	• Evaluate and select partners who are values-aligned.
	• Create measures of success.
	• Proactively mitigate bias.
	• Be sure you are protecting users' data privacy.
Go	• Create an iterative implementation process beginning with a prototype to pressure test your use case concept.
	• Set up a pilot test with small number of end users, gather feedback, and revise.
	• Make go/no-go decision.
	• Ensure you have in-house capacity to sustain and scale effective use over time.

READY

Readiness begins with identifying real and important problems people are having inside and outside of your organization. The most common mistake organizations make is using a smart tech hammer and then looking around for nails. As Nick Hamlin, director of Data Science and Analytics at Global Giving, told us, "AI is like hot sauce. A little bit, used in the right place, can be perfect. But dumping too much on or using it everywhere will probably ruin your meal."[2] In strategic terms, this means pinpointing the exact problem to be addressed.

Identifying Pain Points with the Stakeholder Team

The starting point for organizations is identifying the needs of people who will administer and be affected by the systems and their pain points. There are some common pain points we have heard internal stakeholders like staff and external stakeholders like clients say.

Internal Stakeholders:

- "We don't have enough people to keep up with client demands."

- "We spend more time doing paperwork than serving clients."

- "We spend hours manually going through records to find the right information for our clients."

- "We spend an enormous amount of time gathering and researching information about existing and prospective donors."

- "We keep answering the same questions over and over again on the phone."

- "We keep typing in the same answers into emails or live chat even though the information is on our website."

- "We don't have a translator to talk to clients."

- "The donor said no because we didn't cultivate them before the ask."

- "There was no way for us to know that the client was at risk."

External Stakeholders:

- "I had to wait hours on hold to find out the status of my application and benefits."

- "We don't have water due to the storm, and I need to know where to get bottled water right now."

- "I found a missing dog but can't locate its owner to return it."

- "I'm not a lawyer and don't understand whether I can sue my landlord."

- "I'm in a crisis and just need someone to talk to."

- "Will my donation be processed in euros or dollars?"

- "I would consider donating to this organization again, but no one has talked to me in years."

- "I tried to make a donation online, but something went wrong and no one was available to answer my question."

You may have systems in place to get general feedback from internal and external users. You can use that feedback as a starting point in identifying pain points. We suggest creating a team of stakeholders to help you define a strategic, mission-driven purpose and determine how smart tech might help address those pain points in a clear problem statement. Keep in mind that these stakeholders should come from a range of different roles, and they should include frontline members and general workers, not just managers. The team of stakeholders needs to ask the right sorts of questions to help identify the pain points that smart tech might help address. Here are some guiding questions to help you identify your particular pain points:

- Do we have data about this pain point or is it just a general feeling? (And if it's just a general feeling, you should get data!)

- Is this a problem smart tech is good at solving? Meaning, is it a problem that happens over and over for which we have (or can create) clear answers?

- What is our current approach to solving this problem? What are the current limitations?

- Which stakeholders (internal/external) will be affected by a change in how we do this?

- What unintended consequences might exist for end users? What are the potential harms? What do our ethical advisors think?

Use Cases

Moving from pain points to solutions requires use cases. A use case is a brief narrative description of who will use the technology, how they will use it, and any other important issues we need to consider along with the implementation of smart tech.

Here are a few examples of use cases:

Example #1: Our major gifts team is spending too much time doing "desk research" (researching and prioritizing potential donors and developing a cultivation schedule) and not enough time meeting with donors. We need to automate the process of reviewing thousands of unstructured notes and giving history and providing the best list of prospects. This will help enable us to spend more time strengthening our relationships with existing and prospective donors, avoid donors falling through the cracks, and reduce uncompensated overtime for staff.

Example #2: The demand for answers to client questions outstrips our capacity to answer them. We want to redirect staff time from answering rote questions to building relationships with clients. A chatbot will help automate the process of answering the questions, freeing up staff to spend more time on the human aspects of working with our clients. We need to determine what questions should be automated and when clients should be directed to a person.

Example #3: Handwritten applications require too much time to decipher and retype into our system. We could save an enormous amount of staff time by automating our application process. It would get information into our system faster and help reduce the wait time for benefits from clients.

Example #4: There is far greater demand for our counseling services than we have trained counselors. We can train more counselors using an automated training system that involves simulated conversations. However, we will never allow bots to actually do counseling with our clients.

Example #5: Robots are reliable and safe alternatives to volunteers for packing food boxes and doing inventory in our food bank. However, volunteers are the heart of our organization, and we must find new ways for them to engage in our services and help clients.

The User Journey Map

An agreed-upon use case is then turned into a user journey map, a step-by-step outline of the end users' experience. An exercise like this is particularly important for public-facing tools like chatbots. The user journey outlines the questions a client might ask a chatbot and the corresponding responses. It also identifies exactly where automation ends and human interaction begins.

Table 7.2 provides a simplified example of a user journey for a chatbot designed to answer questions about hurricanes by a disaster response organization.

Table 7.2   User Journey Example

User Profile	Types of Questions	Answers
Affected by Disaster	Needs help with a life-threatening situation—road to house is flooded and they can't get out. Electric wires are down. Stressed out and traumatized by experience.	Route to human or call 911.
Affected by Disaster	Needs the locations of where to get clean water, food, and other supplies.	Provide a list with addresses, phone numbers, and hours.
Wants to Help	Wants to donate.	Provide a link to landing page.
	Wants to volunteer.	Provide a page with a list of volunteer opportunities.

Chris Tuttle is an advisor to nonprofits on their digital strategies. He recently helped a food bank transition from a live chat function to a chatbot. A live chat requires a person to respond in real time to messages. The demand created by the pandemic made this an impossible task. The live chat notification bell was going off constantly, indicating that another person or family needed help. This was more than a distraction; the manifestation of hunger and despair through a constantly ringing bell was taking an emotional toll on staff.[3]

The team responded by creating a user journey map. To do this, they reviewed the live chat transcript to analyze what types of questions were appropriate to answer by a chatbot and which clients should be routed to a human to respond. They explored in detail all the actions and tasks that the chatbot could do best and what the human does best and precisely where the hand-off should be.

CHECKLIST FOR THE READY STEP

Your organization needs to test the assumptions based on internal discussions about the pain points, use cases, and the user journey. You'll need to tailor your approach to the needs of your organization, but a good starting point would be to do these tasks:

Task: Involve end users through interviews or observations to define the problem from their point of view.

- What stakeholders can you interview or observe to gather more information about the problem?

- What questions will you ask them?

- How will you interview them?

- Based on the interview notes, do our stake-holders or end users view this pain point as the right problem to solve or has something else emerged?

- Do you need to revise your description of the pain points?

Task: Test your use cases.

- Do your proposed use cases match what you heard from end users?

- What are some potential new use cases based on end user feedback?

- Can you describe how your pain point might be solved by smart tech from their point of view?

Task: Create a user journey map.

- What is the user journey to reach your goal? Is this a good experience or one filled with frustration or potential harm to the end user if not routed to a human?

- What tasks or decisions will be automated and what tasks or decisions will only be done by humans?

- Does the work flow align with our values in the way we treat our people?

(continued)

(*continued*)

Task: Identify unintended consequences.

- Would automating this task pose a barrier to building relationships and trust with clients or donors?

- Are there feedback loops built into the technology to help people understand how it is working?

- Based on user feedback, is there the potential for the use cases to have unintended consequences? What are the unintended consequences? How can you iterate on your use case to mitigate risk?

Set

It is critically important to be a savvy and skeptical consumer of smart tech. If you have access to tech and legal experts, this is a good place to have them weigh in on your choices. There are three areas to explore at this stage: selecting the right vendor, potential bias, and protecting users' privacy.

Selecting a Vendor

It's important to carefully examine smart tech products or services you are considering using. Here are questions you can ask individual potential vendors you are considering:

- What is your process for selecting a vendor?

- How does your technology align with our core values? Do these smart technology vendors align with our nonprofit's values?

- How will the technology help us solve our end user's problem and achieve better outcomes?

- How has the vendor or solution solved this problem with other nonprofits? How did the nonprofit/vendor measure success? What were the measurable results?

- What does the research literature say about the effectiveness of this type of technology?

- What capacity do we need in-house to sustain it, or will we be reliant on the vendor to get the work done?

There are two important stumbling blocks to be aware of and avoid at this stage of considering vendors:

Shiny object syndrome: Every generation is mesmerized by the next new technology promoted as the magical solver of all of their problems. Don't get distracted from your purpose and values by the latest off-the-shelf product. The goal isn't to use smart tech; the goal is to solve problems in thoughtful, values-aligned ways.

Black boxes: Commercial software vendors most often consider the algorithms that power their tools proprietary. It is their "secret sauce" and how they make money. These secretive, opaque products are often derisively called "black boxes." It will be difficult to avoid black boxes when working with vendors. But you are not obliged to just go along with their assurances. If you are going to use one that will substitute for human decision-making, you are obliged to try to pry them open just a bit and ask important questions to decide if this product is worthy of your organization.

Mitigating Bias

A critically important part of your process is to look carefully for bias built into the training data or system. This may be where you have to bang hard on a black box and ask questions of a potentially reluctant commercial vendor about whether and how the system has been tested for bias. The willingness or unwillingness of a vendor to engage with you in this process will tell you a lot about their values.

Questions to ask about potential biases in the data are:

- What data were used to train the system?
- If third-party data is being used, where does it originate?
- How were data labels assigned and what are the definitions?
- Where and how might bias creep into the system?

Algorithms can also also be biased. It is important scrutinize algorithms for potential bias using these questions:

- Who designed the code and algorithms?
- Did they get input from subject matter experts on the problem it is designed to solve?
- What assumptions are built into the code?
- What proxies were used?
- Was the algorithm tested to reduce bias?

Data Privacy

The privacy of end users has to be a top-tier concern. If data is being captured about individuals, is it being anonymized? It is important to ask these data privacy questions:

- If the data is being captured, is it being anonymized? Has personally identifiable information (PII) from data sets been removed, so that the people whom the data describe are anonymous?

- Who owns the data? Where is it housed?

- Is there an outside ethics committee charged with reviewing the product for privacy and bias?

- What is your company's data-use and privacy pledge?

Once you have asked and answered these questions, you are ready to begin an iterative process of implementation.

Go

At this point, you've finished identifying your goals, creating your plan, and preparing your vendors and tools, and you're ready to start using smart tech. Thoughtful implementation begins with a couple of baby steps to test whether there is a solid footing before it takes off running. This means starting with prototypes and pilot tests, reaching a go/no-go decision, and then launching into a full-scale implementation.

Prototypes and Pilot Tests

Using smart tech is a big decision, and we strongly recommend an implementation process that includes prototyping as well as a pilot testing with a small group of users before full-scale launch. If the model works as expected, this kind of careful and thoughtful scaling process causes no harm. However, if there are, say, problems of bias or the results aren't what was promised, scaling this way will save an enormous amount of heartache. Working this way requires tight coordination between technical and program staff people.

A prototype tests a design element, idea, or assumption for staff and end users. It can demonstrate functionality in the real world. For instance, a prototype for a chatbot could give you feedback on whether and how your end users will respond to an automated approach.

A pilot test is a trial run of the smart technology with a small and controlled sample of end users. The purpose of running a pilot is to get a good understanding of how the smart tech works at full scale before going to full launch. Methods for assessing pilot tests include observation, interviews, and user reviews.

Arriving at Go or No-Go

It is not a guarantee that pilot testing will lead to full implementation. Choosing not to go forward is as important an outcome as going forward as planned.

Here are two examples of smart tech implementation; one which resulted in a "go" decision and one a "no go." The first examines how Puerto Rico dealt with the Zika outbreak in 2017, and the second explores how the Best Friends Animal Society sought to increase animal adoptions.

The Zika virus outbreak in 2017 was an enormous health crisis in Puerto Rico. Puerto Ricans lacked accurate health information about Zika and were skeptical about the gravity of the virus. Public health officials, in partnership with IDEO, decided to quickly prototype and pilot test Zikabot, a chatbot for Puerto Ricans to ask anonymous questions about Zika and receive accurate and timely health information.

They prototyped with a small group of users who texted their questions to Zikabot, which a team of subject experts answered. In some cases, the team debated internally on the most appropriate answers.

Prototyping confirmed many of the team's assumptions. It demonstrated the public's lack of basic knowledge about the virus. It showed how a simple bot could distribute accurate public health information and track the questions that were top of mind for the public. The team also learned that a more conversational approach was required because formally worded responses created distrust. Finally, it became apparent that the anonymity of the chatbot emboldened users to ask far more personal and revealing questions than they did in person. After updating the code and script based on these findings, Zikabot was fully and successfully launched.[4]

The mission of Best Friends Animal Society is to make the country no-kill by 2025 by increasing adoption rates. They partnered with Microsoft's social chatbot Zo to reach new people and share the benefits of pet adoption. The "Black Cat Adoption Week Campaign" was chosen as Zo's pilot run to try to overcome the old superstition about black cats being bad luck.

Sue Citro, Best Friends' chief experience officer, recalled, "We started with a script for Zo that talked about how black cats are great companions and how Zo found them so cute. But we also identified a red flag during the prototype stage that it would be easy to teach Zo to repeat racial slurs or inappropriate sexual innuendos or maybe very direct ones using a different word instead of cat." Continues Citro, "We had to spend more time training her on what *not* to say before doing a pilot." Zo promoted some black cats over others during prototyping. Citro thinks it was because the programmer took a liking to those particular cats. This illustrates how easy it is for a coder to embed their personal opinions into the code. Nontechnical testers caught this bias, a good reminder of the need to have open, participatory processes for designing and testing smart tech.

Ultimately, Zo has been retired and no other animal campaigns were co-piloted. Says Citro, "Because of how much time was needed to ensure the bot didn't learn and share inappropriate ideas and words, we paused these newer strategies and pursued more direct life-saving work with the animals."[5]

Going Full-Scale and Maintenance

Going to full scale requires internal capacity to manage the tech in a sustainable way. Anna Bethke, head of AI for social good at Intel AI Products Group, said, "Artificial intelligence projects require constant attention. It isn't a 'set it and forget it.' In some cases, there have been capacity issues with deployment because a proper staffing plan wasn't established."[6]

You may not have the capacity to hire a dedicated staff person to manage smart tech. However, existing staff people can be supported to develop the knowledge and skills necessary through education and training. In addition, there are volunteers with technical expertise available through organizations like DataKind or technology companies.

Tasks for smooth scaling and maintenance include:

- Regular testing of results for bias.
- Regular maintenance and updating of your data set and algorithm.
- Regular check-ins with vendors to see what, if anything, has changed with their models and what they are learning.
- Interviews with users and stakeholders to monitor how well the smart tech is solving the intended problems, and what, if any, new problems it may be creating.
- Regular reports to senior executives and boards on the process and outcomes of smart tech use.
- Plans for next phases or additional functionality and scaling infrastructure.

CONCLUSION

Getting ready should not be taken lightly or skipped. Take your time, do not rush, and give your organization the permission to hit the pause button if there is any potential to do harm. We've included key questions in this chapter to help you determine whether your organization has assessed unintended consequences at every preparation step along the way.

ENDNOTES

1. Author interview with Leila Toplic May 22, 2021.
2. Author interview with Nick Hamlin, July 3, 2020.
3. Chris Tuttle, Facebook post: https://www.facebook.com/the christuttle/posts/10164903078310307.

4. David Boardman, "Zikabot—Prototyping a Chatbot To Build Empathy with the Communities Affected by Zika in Puerto Rico," (http://www.thedavidboardman.com/p-zikabot.php).

5. Interview with Sue Citro, July 30, 2021.

6. Interview with Anna Bethke, July 30, 2019.

CHAPTER 8

Automating Program Delivery

INTRODUCTION

The reason nonprofit organizations exist is to provide a service or raise awareness of an issue. Everything else that happens such as fundraising, communications, accounting, and human resources is in service of those programs. One of the most important applications of smart tech is to support the delivery of services. This chapter outlines the ways smart tech is adding capacity to serve and support people, triaging clients in crisis, and supporting advocacy efforts.

CREATING MORE CAPACITY

It is a heartbreaking reality of social service providers that demand constantly outstrips supply. Smart tech may never be able to solve this problem, but it can help mitigate it by augmenting staff efforts. The pandemic was a catalyst for accelerated adoption of smart tech to create more organizational capacity to provide information and services.

Doctors Without Borders/Médecins Sans Frontières (MSF) is an international humanitarian group dedicated to providing medical care to people in distress, including victims of political violence and natural disasters. The organization has been a leader in using smart tech to deliver services. Before 2020, the organization had used chatbots successfully to answer questions on its website that averages 10,000 visits a day. When COVID-19 hit, the organization expanded on this success by creating a chatbot to answer questions about the pandemic. Nick Scott, head of digital for MSF, said, "We noticed a huge increase in conversations within our social media community around mental health, anxiety, and other well-being issues. We started to produce new material with MSF's psychological support units and their experience in other epidemics that could help website visitors during this difficult period."[1]

Food scarcity skyrocketed during the pandemic. City Harvest and the Greater Boston Food Bank partnered with automation expert Berkshire Grey to provide a Thanksgiving meal to over 12,000 people. Robots packed the meals.[2]

COVID-19 also created a profound problem for children who rely on school lunches. With distance learning in place, students were not able to receive meals. The system was designed for clients to come for the food, not for food to go to clients. Researchers at Carnegie Mellon used machine learning to tackle this problem in the Pittsburgh area. Karen Lightman of Carnegie Mellon said, "When COVID closed schools in March and disrupted meal programs around the region, we pivoted. Instead of buses carrying students, we developed a program to have drivers bring lunches to families most in need." All new bus routes were created to maximize their efficiency in delivering meals. This is a fantastic example other municipalities could adopt for service delivery of all kinds.[3]

In addition to augmenting program capacity, smart tech can help build the knowledge and skills of individual staffers. The Africa chapter of Nethope, a membership organization focused on using tech for good, created "Mama Africa." The chatbot shares technical information between local members. Previously members were providing just-in-time technical support to their peers and advice by email and WhatsApp. Anyone who has participated in a listserv, group text, or Facebook group with professional colleagues knows how difficult it can be to find the right information or resources from past conversations. Mama Africa provides advice on a wide range of technical topics using video training modules and text-based answers to frequently asked questions. It also provides connections to local organizations and allows users to contribute content, capabilities beyond most chatbots.[4]

OVERCOMING SERVICE BARRIERS

An enormous pain point for service providers is ensuring they are providing the right services to the right people in a timely way. For example, public defenders are typically overwhelmed with client cases. They generally juggle 80 to 100 cases a week. A programmer, Darrell Malone Jr., saw this pain point and created The Tubman Project Toolkit to help ease the burden on public defenders and "help make a dent into the problem of mass incarceration."[5] The open-source suite of tools automates rote tasks generally done by a paralegal. The tools include an automatic brief filer and a tool to help identify video footage from security cameras or body camera video captures. Finding the right footage used to take hours compared to the automation algorithms that can zero in on the right bits in seconds.

Automating routine and time-consuming paperwork by enabling clients to fill out forms themselves frees up defenders to focus on preparing a better legal case. John Mayer, executive director, Center for Computer-Assisted Legal Instruction/CALI, who has over thirty years of experience working on technology for the legal services field, says, "We want lawyers to practice at the top of their license and that isn't doing the basic intake or filing forms. This is where automation with expert systems can give legal professionals more time to deal with their clients' emotions, be more empathetic, and be a better lawyer."[6]

Another example of automating paperwork comes from Joshua Browder, a Stanford University student. He designed the DoNotPay bot initially to help drivers appeal parking fines. Then, he recalled, "I began to get really heartfelt emails relating to evictions, bankruptcies, and other situations, and at the time I felt bad I couldn't help. That made me decide to expand this to help homeless people."[7]

The bot asks homeless people a few standard questions— where they live, whether they are eligible for government housing, the circumstances surrounding their homelessness, and whether they have been diagnosed with a physical or mental health issue. A completed application designed to increase an applicant's odds of being placed in a home is generated. If an individual has a physical disability, for example, the bot will rearrange the application to focus on that condition.[8]

One of the most exciting areas for automation is a single bot's ability to understand and converse in many different languages. Overcoming language barriers is critically important for ensuring information is accurately delivered, particularly healthcare information.

Translators without Borders (TWB) in partnership with Mercy Corps developed a chatbot named Shehu, a word meaning scholar in the Nigerian dialects of Hausa and Kanuri. The chatbot converses in three languages to improve COVID-19 understanding in northeast Nigeria. The chatbot allows users to ask questions in their native language and receive answers immediately and conversationally. The chatbot is fluent in English, Hausa, and

Kanuri, languages used in the region. The chatbot provides accurate answers to questions such as: "How can I catch COVID-19?"; "If I feel sick, what should I do?"; and "Can vaccines prevent me from infecting others with COVID-19?"[9]

In addition to providing information, Shehu is helping to identify gaps in information. Program staff people access a dashboard that tracks what questions are being asked and how frequently as well as what languages are being used most often. This information shapes program delivery and communications strategy.

Smart tech isn't just helping people receive services. Animal shelters are also adopting smart technologies. Companion Labs is experimenting with dog-training robots in partnership with the San Francisco SPCA. The CompanionPro trainer uses a variety of smart tech technologies to train on commands like "sit." It even delivers cookies as rewards.[10]

We met the Best Friends Animal Society in Chapter 7, "Ready, Set, Go." The organization is using smart tech apps to help increase adoption rates. Most shelters put photos of the animals available for adoption online along with descriptions so potential adopters can self-select their preferred match. Photos showing off the animal's endearing qualities are critical to increasing the adoption rates.

However, photos taken by volunteers are often not of great quality. That's where Adoptimize comes in.[11] Volunteers use the app to take photos. The app's algorithm extracts the best photo for posting and removes the shelter cage background. The app has been tested widely and is increasing adoption rates.

Smart tech is also being used to find lost pets. Shadow, an AI-powered app, helps owners find their lost pets by matching them with social media images.[12]

CRISIS INTERVENTION

Triaging clients and patients to ensure that the most urgent cases are treated first is a matter of life and death. Suicide rates of veterans have been rising at alarming rates for the last several years. Currently more than 20 vets take their own lives each day. Traditionally, doctors diagnose a patient's risk based on a physical examination and interview, review of their charts, and using their expertise and experience. Dr. Marianne S. Goodman, a psychiatrist at the Veterans Integrated Service Network in the Bronx, said, "The fact is, we can't rely on trained medical experts to identify people who are truly at high risk, because those patients are the least likely to go to the doctor."

To help identify vets at greatest risk of self-harm, the Department of Veterans Affairs turned to smart tech.[13] The Reach Vet algorithm was trained to analyze sixty-one factors most closely associated with suicide risks from thousands of previous suicides in the VA's database over the past decade.[14] An overall index score was then developed for each vet, with the top 0.01% deemed the highest risk, requiring immediate attention.

The algorithm searches health and social service agency records for patterns that are associated with suicide. When the system flags a vet, their name is sent to the local clinic's Reach Vet coordinator who works with the client to create a prevention strategy and provide access to support resources. It is important to note that the "high-risk designation" is a warning sign, not a prophecy, which is why the bot is matched with a social worker to ensure that each person is treated with individual care.

Suicide is also the second leading cause of death for young people of ages 10 to 24.[15] Crisis Text Line began as a hotline for young people experiencing mental health crises. In a study examining emergency room suicide assessments, teens were more like to report thoughts of suicide verbally on social media and by text messages than to a doctor.

Crisis Text Line uses smart tech as part of the intake process to immediately identify people who are at the highest risk. Automating the intake process ensures that volunteers are interacting with people in need rather than spending time coding or tagging or storing data. The overall approach is deeply human-centered as every interaction after the automated intake process is with a person.[16,17]

There is another quiet health crisis in the country: loneliness. It is particularly acute for homebound seniors. The problem is becoming an epidemic because older adults make up the fastest growing demographic in the country, and 43% of Americans over sixty identify as lonely. This will be compounded by the estimated shortfall of 151,000 paid care workers in the US in the next decade.

Robots are on the way to help reduce the despair and host of medical problems exacerbated by loneliness. These "social robots" monitor an older person's health and activities. The robots can also integrate with other smart tech in the home and provide information, read a book, and answer the phone.[18,19,20]

REMOVING BARRIERS TO ACCESSIBILITY

Smart tech is creating access to services for people with disabilities. Many examples exist of how the technology can remove barriers:

- Image recognition for people with a visual impairment.
- Facial recognition for people with a visual impairment.

- Lip-reading recognition for people with a hearing impairment.

- Text summarization for people with a mental impairment.

- Real-time captioning or translations for people with a hearing impairment or even people who don't speak the language.[21]

Microsoft reports that "AI can empower people with disabilities with tools that support independence and productivity, as technology rapidly changes the way we live, learn, and work."[22] This work includes chatbots for people with visual challenges, improving real-time captioning for the hearing impaired, and chatbots to provide explanatory help. Of course, any use of AI to expand accessibility for staff can be extended to help provide accessibility for clients and other constituents.

Smart tech can also help people with disabilities become staff people. The Dawn Avatar Robot Café in Japan features robots waiting on customers and serving food and drink. It's not a gimmick, though. These robots are operated remotely via the internet, serving as avatars for people who can't leave the house for long periods of time due to physical disabilities, childcare, or for other reasons. Company cofounder and CEO Kentaro Yoshifuji got the idea to design remote-controlled robot waiters after his own experience of being bedridden in the hospital for the greater part of three years.[23]

ADVOCACY

In addition to direct program delivery, nonprofit organizations are beginning to use smart tech for advocacy efforts by raising awareness and educating the public about issues. Feeding America, the largest domestic hunger-relief and food rescue organization, wanted to "show" people what hunger looks like. In partnership with the Ad Council and Leo Burnett, they created a public service campaign called, "I am Hunger in America."[24] They gathered thousands of photos of clients (with permission) and fed this data into facial recognition software. This information was compared to national data regarding the demographics of food insecurity, which helped narrow down the photo set to 1000. Finally, one composite face was created to illustrate what hunger "looks" like in America. The myth-busting result shows that hunger looks like a white woman, who likely has children.

We have already introduced you to Rita Ko and her United Nations innovation unit called HIVE. Rita and her colleagues have been battling all of the hatred, xenophobia, and racism aimed at refugees for years. In 2017, they began analyzing enormous amounts of data about public attitudes in order to try to shift attitudes toward refugees in a positive direction. Ko said, "The refugee crisis is polarizing. There is a lot of noise and strong feelings around the crisis. In collaboration with DataKind, we developed an algorithm that sweeps through 44 news media outlets and any stories they publish on refugees or immigration. We use natural language processing, a machine learning technique, to generate a summary of topics and sentiments of individual news stories. The report is automatically shared . . . with our communications and fundraising teams so they can figure out how to change the conversation or develop messaging that will help convert or acquire new supporters."[25]

Analyzing public understanding of issues is more complex than conducting a public opinion survey. It includes analyzing what people are saying about the issue on social media channels as well as analysis of media coverage. Harmony Labs has developed the infrastructure to identify, measure, and track narratives over long time scales and connect them to people.[26]

Harmony Labs created Project Ariel to examine public narratives around climate change. Using social network analysis from over 26,000 Twitter accounts and a large number of conversations on the social networking site Reddit, the project produced a nuanced snapshot of climate skeptic conversations. The research has been shared in small briefings to inform climate change communicators looking to broaden their reach beyond existing supporters.

CONCLUSION

There may be no more important use for smart tech for nonprofits than using it to expand the capacity of staff and provide access to all people. This is an area where co-botting becomes particularly important to ensure that staff and clients stay at the center of services with smart tech providing support. The results will be an enormous expansion of the number of people served and, hopefully, an equal increase in the quality of those services and efforts.

ENDNOTES

1. Pedro Marque, "The need behind the need of Médecins Sans Frontières," Landbot website, https://landbot.io/customer-stories/medecins-sans-frontieres.
2. "Robotics Innovator Berkshire Grey Announces Picking with Purpose Program to Provide Food to 4000 Families This Thanksgiving," *Robotics Tomorrow* (November 19, 2020), https://www.roboticstomorrow.com/news/2020/11/19/robotics-innovator-berkshire-grey-announces-picking-with-purpose-program-to-provide-food-to-4000-families-this-thanksgiving/15945/.

3. Jessica Kent, "Machine Learning Helps Reduce Food Insecurity During COVID-19," *Health IT Analytics* (November 6, 2020), https://healthitanalytics.com/news/machine-learning-helps-reduce-food-insecurity-during-covid-19.

4. Nethope Blog, "Chatbots Made in Africa: Collective Action and Lessons Learned" (May 26, 2021), https://nethope.org/2021/05/26/chatbots-made-in-africa-collective-action-and-lessons-learned/.

5. Author interview with Darrell Malone, July 3, 2021.

6. Author interview with John Mayer on June 23, 2021.

7. Tiffany Fishman, William D. Eggers, and Pankaj Kamleshkumar Kishnani, "AI-augmented human services: using cognitive technologies to transform program delivery," Deloitte (October 17, 2017), https://www2.deloitte.com/us/en/insights/industry/public-sector/artificial-intelligence-technologies-human-services-programs.html/#endnote-14.

8. Tiffany Fishman, William D. Eggers, and Pankaj Kamleshkumar Kishnani, "AI-augmented human services: using cognitive technologies to transform program delivery," Deloitte (October 17, 2017), https://www2.deloitte.com/us/en/insights/industry/public-sector/artificial-intelligence-technologies-human-services-programs.html/#endnote-14.

9. TWB Communications, "TWB develops language technology to improve humanitarian communication in northeast Nigeria" (April 7, 2021), https://translatorswithoutborders.org/chatbot-release-northeast-nigeria/.

10. Brian Cooley, "Help dogs deal with separation anxiety with this AI trainer," CNET (November 25, 2020), https://www.cnet.com/home/smart-home/help-dogs-deal-with-separation-anxiety-with-this-ai-trainer/.

11. Adoptimize Animal Shelter Software, https://www.adoptimize.co, August 26, 2021.

12. Samantha Barlett, DVM, "Shelters Use AI to Help Find Owners of Rescued Dogs" (March 1, 2021), http://www.kcvma.com/2021/03/01/shelters-use-ai-to-help-find-owners-of-rescued-dogs/.

13. Benedict Carey, "Can an Algorithm Prevent Suicide?," *New York Times* (November 23, 2020), https://www.nytimes.com/2020/11/23/health/artificial-intelligence-veterans-suicide.html.

14. Mike Richmanm, "Study evaluates VA program that identifies vets at highest risk for suicide," US Department of Veteran Affairs, Office of Research & Development (September 20, 2018), https://www.research.va.gov/currents/0918-Study-evaluates-VA-program-that-identifies-Vets-at-highest-risk-for-suicide.cfm.

15. National Suicide Prevention Lifeline, Youth, August 26, 2021, https://suicidepreventionlifeline.org/help-yourself/youth/.

16. Allison Fine and Beth Kanter, "Leveraging the Power of Bots for Civil Society," Stanford Social Innovation Review blog (April 11, 2018), https://ssir.org/articles/entry/leveraging_the_power_of_bots_for_civil_society.

17. Crisis Text Line website, August 26, 2021, https://www.crisistextline.org/.

18. Katie Engelhart, "What Robots Can—and Can't—Do for the Old and Lonely," *New Yorker Magazine* (May 24, 2021), https://www.newyorker.com/magazine/2021/05/31/what-robots-can-and-cant-do-for-the-old-and-lonely.

19. Barry Sardis, "How Can Social Robots Help the Elderly Age in Place Better and Longer?," TechforAging (July 16, 2020), https://techforaging.com/social-robots-elderly/.

20. Corinne Purtill, "Stop Me If You've Heard This One: A Robot and a Team of Irish Scientists Walk Into a Senior Living Home," *Time Magazine* (October 4, 2019), https://time.com/longform/senior-care-robot/.

21. Carole Martinez, "Artificial Intelligence and Accessibility: Examples of a Technology that Serves People with Disabilities" (March 5, 2021), https://www.inclusivecitymaker.com/artificial-intelligence-accessibility-examples-technology-serves-people-disabilities/.

22. "Microsoft, AI even more accessible," *Digital News Tech* (May 13, 2021), https://digitalnewtech.com/en/2021/05/13/microsoft-ai-even-more-accessible/.

23. Emma Steen, "This new Tokyo café has robot waiters controlled remotely by disabled workers," Time Out (June 22, 2021), (https://www.timeout.com/tokyo/news/this-new-tokyo-cafe-has-robot-waiters-controlled-remotely-by-disabled-workers-021621.

24. "I am Hunger in America," Feeding America website (August 26, 2021), https://www.feedingamerica.org/i-am-hunger/chapter/how).

25. Author interview with Rita Ko on August 1, 2020, and originally published in "Scaling Generosity Report" by Allison Fine and Beth Kanter, March 30, 2020.

26. Harmony Labs website (August 26, 2021), https://harmonylabs .org/.

CHAPTER 9

Fundraising

INTRODUCTION

Fundraising is a particularly promising area for smart tech to help staff become better and smarter fundraisers, but it also holds great peril by potentially supersizing existing bad practices.[1] This chapter will provide a brief history of how and why transactional fundraising became the norm for too many organizations and the ways that smart tech can help organizations identify new donors, personalize fundraising for all donors, and improve retention rates.

THE LEAKY BUCKET PROBLEM

Conventional wisdom says that finding new low dollar donors will lose money, but that money will be more than made up in the subsequent years. This isn't true. Sometimes wisdom is conventional and wrong.

There is an enormous, malignant, too often ignored problem in fundraising created by the impersonal treatment of donors. We call it the leaky bucket problem. Far more donors lapse than renew their donations, causing a frantic race to find new donors to fill up the bucket. Acquiring new donors does, indeed, lose money, often estimated at 50% of the initial gift.[2] However, according to Blackbaud, fewer than a quarter of those initial donors will renew their gift. The math gets even worse in out-years, as 60% of donors lapse year after year.

Here are facts about the leaky bucket problem:

- Fewer than a quarter of donors renew their gift a second time.

- 60% of donors lapse every year thereafter. Until . . .

- After five years, just 10% of the original donors are left.

- Contrary to conventional wisdom, acquiring new donors not only loses a lot of money initially, estimated at 50% of the initial gift, it is not recouped in the out-years.[3]

- It costs seven times more money to acquire a new donor than renew an existing one.

This is not a new problem. Adrian Sargeant, one of the world's leading philanthropic researchers, said, "The donor retention landscape is actually lousy at the moment and is going . . . from bad to worse." He didn't say that in 2020; he said it in 2013 when the US economy was at its most robust moment in a generation.[4] This is corroborated by the Fundraising Effectiveness Project, which has data showing that poor donor retention rates have pretty much stayed the same since 2005.[5]

The leaky bucket problem turns good fundraisers into frantic ones and burns them out. The leaky bucket problem drives a transactional approach to fundraising that requires constantly asking for donations rather than spending time getting to know donors, particularly donors who aren't writing huge checks. This problem is pervasive across issue areas and size of organizations.

There was hope that the internet and social media could fix the leaky bucket problem by making person-to-person connecting, sharing, communicating, and organizing easy and inexpensive at scale—with or without organizations as intermediaries. Social media enabled efforts like GivingTuesday, a worldwide phenomenon of organizations and people raising money for causes the Tuesday after Thanksgiving. It has benefited enormously from the network effect, digital tech that enables the dramatic spread of information without organizations having to do all the heavy lifting themselves.

Person-to-person platforms like GoFundMe also gained popularity by enabling direct giving to people rather than to organizations: to, say, cover extraordinary expenses arising from a medical crisis. GoFundMe has become the largest crowdfunding platform in the world—50 million people gave more than $5 billion on the site through 2017.[6]

In 2015, Facebook opened up its platform for direct fundraising appeals. According to a Facebook press release, over $2 billion has been raised on Facebook, with $1 billion raised from birthday fundraisers alone; and 45 million people having donated to or created a fundraiser of their own, a number that doubled in 2020.[7]

And yet, even though the origins were different, and often friends were involved in the initial raise, these small dollar donors went into the same leaky bucket as their direct mail predecessors with automated email thank-you letters and subsequent barrage of urgent requests asking for a donation right now, today, before the sky falls. The normal return for solicitations like these is around 5%.[8] This means that 95% of the recipients didn't respond and either tuned out the cause or were mildly annoyed or furious and unsubscribed. Is that really how organizations should want people to view their cause?

There has always been a parallel track for the treatment of high dollar donors, people giving, say, $500 or more to a cause. These donors often receive a personal thank-you note or call, invitations to briefings by the chief executive with fellow donors, and a seat at the front table for the annual gala. And if your teenager is looking for an internship for the summer, well, it's likely a big donation can help facilitate that, too.

It isn't rational to keep pouring donors into leaky buckets, and yet the problem persists. Why? One reason is because of what happens inside the boardroom. We have served on many boards during our careers and been present at many, many board meetings, and have never heard a discussion about the leaky bucket problem. Not once. Presentations by the development team are generally a snapshot of progress against current fiscal year budgets. This makes sense. As fiduciary agents, the most basic responsibility of board members is to ensure the financial well-being of the organization.

The issues we've never heard discussed include:

- How many donors, or potential donors, did we lose this year from our appeals?

- Have we talked personally to any low dollar donors who didn't renew their gifts to ask why they didn't renew?

- Did that very expensive donor acquisition campaign last year and the year before actually recoup the investment this year?

Organizational leaders need to grapple with the root causes of the leaky bucket problem before introducing smart tech into fundraising systems or risk exacerbating them instead of fixing them.

USING SMART TECH FOR RELATIONAL FUNDRAISING

Smart tech creates the opportunity to create a new bucket, a solid one without any leaks. Kevin Bromer, former vice president of product delivery for Salesforce/Nonprofit Cloud, said, "The era of spray and pray fundraising campaigns and strategy will be gone." This may be an overly optimistic statement, but the promise is real. Smart tech brings with it the ability to accumulate knowledge and identify patterns across millions of data points quickly and then precisely match the interests of donors with the work of organizations and unleash a new era of generosity.[9]

Smart tech can help organizations raise money from large numbers of people while giving each donor the kind of personalized experience reserved only for major donors right now. However, this pivot to relational fundraising for all donors is only possible if organizations choose to make the pivot. There is the real and tragic possibility that organizations will use smart tech to supersize transactional fundraising. Brigitte Hoyer Gosselink of Google said, "Smart tech won't fix bad fundraising practices."[10]

We hope organizations will be able to seize this opportunity to fundamentally remake their fundraising culture to focus on connecting with people in real, human ways. Most of all, we hope donors will learn more about causes, feel more connected to them, and stay with them as donors for years, not days.

Smart tech for fundraising is used both to engage existing donors and attract new ones. It augments staff capacity by automating rote tasks such as answering standard donor questions online, research, and customized storytelling. The following sections examine a variety of ways smart tech is changing fundraising.

Donor Prediction Models/Automated Donor Stewardship

Companies such as Blackbaud, boodle.AI, Smarttech, Gravyty, Salesforce, Nonprofit Cloud, and Neon One have products that can automate research about potential donors in minutes. They are literally saving development staff people weeks of work creating prospect lists and organizing meetings. Fundraisers can reallocate this time for face-to-face meetings with donors, learning more about them, building stronger relationships, and personalizing their cultivation.

The donor prediction models can also be leveraged by smaller development offices who are often juggling donor stewardship for corporate sponsors and mid-level donors. NeonMoves, a mobile application, helps fundraisers spend less time figuring out who to contact and more time face-to-face with donors and prospects. The app was originally designed for a national nonprofit's development team who were managing many relationships with corporate sponsors, mid-level, and major donors in many different geographic areas across the country. The mobile app helps make the fundraisers' road trips to visit donors more efficient by identifying other donors to meet while in a particular geographic area, among other tasks.

Customization of Appeals

Smart tech software can customize appeals for donors at every level at a speed and scale far beyond what individuals can do. This is particularly helpful for smaller organizations without large development teams. Smart tech–powered tools can search existing donor bases and the web to identify patterns of interest and past giving by current and potential donors and customize messages for individuals.

Rainforest Action Network took the leap into using smart tech for fundraising in 2020 by working with a software company, Accessible Intelligence Limited. The smart tech system customized stories and appeals to one-time donors in order to convert them into monthly donors. Having predictable income from donors monthly is one of the most valuable assets for organizations. To say their initial results were successful is an understatement. They increased the number of monthly donors by 866% (that's not a typo, really!).

It sounds like magic, but it isn't. Accessible Intelligence's algorithms swam through thousands of entries in their donor history to determine patterns of language and stories to which donors previously responded or had a good chance of responding to in the future. Did they sign petitions before donating? What type of programs or content resonated with them? Did they tend to respond to emergencies or requests to support ongoing programs?

These and hundreds of other data points about supporters' behaviors were labeled and tagged to specific campaign content. The algorithm then made recommendations for what content had the greatest chance to move donors to give.[11]

These kinds of smart tech approaches are creating new methods for classifying donors. Smart tech can predict future behavior such as likelihood to give, likelihood to upgrade their donation, and likelihood to lapse.[12]

Quilt.ai helps nonprofit users move from audience target groups to personalization. The platform indexes and clusters millions of human conversations and expressions across public social media platforms, news sites, blogs, institutional sources, and search engines. It also integrates marketing principles and human behavior models into its model. As Quilt.ai Cofounder and CEO Anurag Banerjee says, "We create a quilt of understanding from trillions of digital fragments." Quilt.ai is aiming to develop a model for predicting future giving behavior. Banerjee notes, "People live in their own 'filter bubbles' and a fundraiser has to understand what motivates and shapes their opinions in order to effectively communicate with them. People give for different reasons and in different contexts. It is important to be digitally empathetic. Otherwise, it is just a scattershot approach."[13]

Persado uses smart tech to analyze the performance of the fundraising creative elements: narrative, emotion, calls-to-action, formatting, and word positioning. It cross-references the words with its database of more than one million tagged and scored words, phrases, and images in 25 languages. It learns continuously and is able to generate insights about what creative materials resonate with donors. Charity: water is using Persado to better understand which content and images on Facebook generate more recurring donors for its monthly giving program.

Real-Time Answers

Extra Life, a gaming marathon created by the Children's Miracle Network Hospitals, has a large number of Canadian participants and donors. They were getting a lot of questions from these supporters about the currency in which their donations would be processed. They added a chatbot to the donation page of Extra Life's site and configured it to show up only for Canadian donors. This way, Canadian constituents could get their questions about currency answered and everyone else's experience was unaffected.

People in general, and gamers in particular, have very short attention spans. It is critically important to ensure that their rote questions can get answered immediately before they move on to another screen or game or task.

Chatbots can be programmed to answer an enormous variety of questions. Whether a user is looking to register at 2 p.m. or 2 a.m., the chatbot is always available. What no organization can afford is to have a potential supporter frustrated that a simple question couldn't be answered immediately.[14]

Automating Workflow

Many fundraising departments miss important opportunities for donor touchpoints such as acknowledging gifts, thanking donors, and other stewardship practices because they are pressed for time and capacity. Smart tech–powered systems can provide reminders, first drafts, and reports, thereby increasing productivity and donor stewardship.

Gravyty is a smart tech tool that drafts communications to donors for review by development staff. Gravyty also drafts donor cultivation plans based on major gift best practices. It can even use data from sources like Yelp to find a restaurant for a donor meeting![15]

Some platforms have created prediction models that identify donors who are in danger of lapsing. This kind of intervention often gets lost in the busyness of everyday life in development offices. Blackbaud's system flags these donors before they lapse to give the organization an opportunity to reach out and renew their giving. Blackbaud automates notifications to nudge the fundraisers to take some action to re-engage donors. For example, it might say, "Sally Smith has had no contact since [date] and is in danger of lapsing."

Increasing Peer-to-Peer Outreach

boodle.AI helps nonprofits find the best potential donors in any list of prospects by using the nonprofit's data along with billions of third-party data points. According to France Q. Hoang, chief strategy officer, "If an algorithm could better understand the peer networks of current donors, it could help the nonprofit bring in new donors."[16]

Blackbaud also provides peer-to-peer strategic help: "Blackbaud . . . creates a network map and analyzes how well-connected prospects are [to each other and the organization]. If an algorithm could better understand the peer networks of current donors, it could help the nonprofit bring in new donors."[17]

THE FUTURE OF GIVING

Kevin Bromer says, "We can imagine 100% response rates because the fundraiser's only sending information to people ready to see it and act on it. That provides a huge ROI along with a better donor experience."[18] Most meetings with donors are built around when and how to make "the ask." What if the point of these meetings wasn't to ask for money, or anything else, but to find out why your cause is so meaningful to a current or prospective donor, who they are as people, and what their aspirations are in life for themselves and their families?

Here are a few ways development (and other) staff could spend their smart tech dividend of time:

> **Share stories.** Ask supporters to tell their stories to you and each other about why your cause is meaningful to them. Ask them when and how you make them inspired or proud (or don't). Encourage them to share their stories with their friends.

Make new friends. Strong, resilient communities don't operate up-and-down but side-to-side. Most organizations operate as hub-and-spoke models with the primary relationship running directly between the organization and a donor. Communities are social networks where people are encouraged to build direct ties to one another. It takes leadership and time to create these new connections, which you now have because of the smart tech dividend of time!

Problem-solve together. Too many organizations go behind closed doors to solve problems. Communal problems need and deserve communally created answers. Organizations need to take their greatest pain points to their communities for discussion. It takes time to educate your community about the problem, why it exists, and what you have done to try to solve it. The final decisions may rest with the staff or board, but there is nothing wrong with engaging a community in real problem solving. Organizations living on the transactional hamster wheel don't have time for this kind of engagement. Scared people and organizations don't ask for help. Confident, bold and brave ones do—be those people.

CONCLUSION

The use of smart tech offers nonprofit fundraisers the opportunity to fix that leaky bucket by being able to spend more time building relationships. Imagine seeing 100% response rates on your donor appeals and sky-high retention rates and never having to stress out about your fundraising goals. No, this isn't a dream—it can be a reality if your organization uses smart tech wisely in the pursuit of lifelong supporters.

ENDNOTES

1. Beth Kanter and Allison Fine, "Scaling Generosity with Artificial Intelligence" (March 30, 2020), https://bit.ly/ai4giving-report.
2. Allison Fine and Beth Kanter, "Rehumanizing Fundraising with Artificial Intelligence," Stanford Social Innovation blog (October 26, 2020), https://ssir.org/articles/entry/re_humanizing_fundraising_with_artificial_intelligence#.
3. True Sense, "Long-Term Value Is a Fundraiser's Most Important Metric. Here's Why!" (October 13, 2017), (https://www.truesense.com/blog/long-term-donor-value-is-a-fundrsmart techsers-most-important-metric.-heres-why).
4. Dr. Adrian Sargeant, "Donor Retention," Bloomerang, October 21, 2013, https://www.youtube.com/watch?v=zc__oMmOmoQ).
5. Fundraising Effective Project, AFP Global website, August 27, 2021, https://afpglobal.org/FundraisingEffectivenessProject.
6. Rachel Monroe, "When GoFundMe Gets Ugly," *The Atlantic* (November 2019), https://www.theatlantic.com/magazine/archive/2019/11/gofundme-nation/598369/.
7. "People Raise Over $2 Billion for Causes on Facebook," Facebook (September 19, 2019), https://about.fb.com/news/2019/09/2-billion-for-causes/.
8. "Analyzing renewal appeal response rates," Smart Annual Giving website, August 27, 2021, https://smartannualgiving.com/appeal-response-rates/.
9. Author interview with Kevin Bromer for Scaling Generosity Report, July 30, 2020.
10. Author interview with Brigitte Hoyer Gosselink for Scaling Generosity Report, July 1, 2020.
11. Accessible Intelligence, "Case Study Rainforest Action Network," August 27, 2021, https://accessibleintelligence.io/resources/case-study-rainforest-action-network/.
12. Tim Paris, "3 AI-Driven KPIs Nonprofits Should Start Tracking," Nonprofit Information, (May 28, 2021), https://nonprofitinformation.com/kpis-nonprofits/.

13. Author interview with Anurag Banerjee, September 15, 2019, for AI4Giving: "Unlocking Generosity with Artificial Intelligence: The Future of Giving" by Beth Kanter and Allison Fine.

14. Extra Life, Children's Miracle Network Hospitals website, https://www.extra-life.org/, August 28, 2021.

15. Gravyty website, https://www.gravyty.com, August 28, 2021.

16. Author interview with France Q. Hoang, September 15, 2019, for AI4Giving: "Unlocking Generosity with Artificial Intelligence: The Future of Giving" by Beth Kanter and Allison Fine.

17. Author interview with Steve MacLaughlin, July, 2019, for AI4Giving: "Unlocking Generosity with Artificial Intelligence: The Future of Giving" by Beth Kanter and Allison Fine.

18. Author interview with Kevin Bromer on August 1, 2019, for AI4Giving: "Unlocking Generosity with Artificial Intelligence: The Future of Giving" by Beth Kanter and Allison Fine.

CHAPTER 10

Automating the Back Office

INTRODUCTION

The back office is where vital administrative tasks that support the inner-workings of nonprofits take place. The activities of the back office are often overlooked and underappreciated, particularly in smaller organizations that may not have the resources for dedicated staff or departments to support these functions. Smart tech systems provide cost effective and efficient ways to support administrators in financial management, human resources, and organizational workflow and project management.

These tools can be a true gift of time for small nonprofits. Even better, many of the products in this category are available off-the-shelf, fairly inexpensive, and somewhat easy to use. This chapter examines the role of smart tech in automating human resources, finance, and workflow and productivity.

HUMAN RESOURCES

A key function of human resources (HR) is ensuring that the right people are in the right jobs. However, HR involves a lot more, including:

- Recruitment and onboarding
- Workplace culture

- Compensation, benefits, and performance review strategy
- Compliance and documentation
- Professional development and training
- Volunteer management

Unfortunately, most mid- to small-sized organizations do not have the resources to have dedicated human resources staff, let alone an entire department. Instead, these important functions are often divided between, say, executive directors building organizational culture, bookkeepers doing payroll and taxes and reporting, and program directors recruiting and managing volunteers. What's lost in the balkanization of these tasks is the overall picture of how people are treated within an organization and whether the right kinds of support exist to help maximize their talents. The incorporation of smart tech has the potential to help organizational leaders lean back from administrative work and lean into the overall picture of human potential and workplace culture within their organizations.

HR is on track to become one of the most automated departments in the organization, particularly for recruitment and screening. According to Mercer's Global Talent Trends 2019 global report, 88% of companies already use automation in some way for HR, with 83% of US employers relying on some form of smart technology for HR.[1]

In particular, chatbots are used to engage with and screen candidates during recruitment. Jill Finlayson, director, Expanding Diversity and Gender Equity in Tech (EDGE in Tech)™ Initiative at the University of California, says, "More and more when an applicant applies for a job, they will likely meet an HR chatbot. These chatbots are designed to collect information from potential applicants, answering questions 24/7, scheduling interviews with humans, chatting by SMS, email, social media, but they may also be asking screening questions. One thing applicants (and many hiring managers) may not know about the software is that it could be filtering applicants in or out depending on how they answer questions and how the algorithm matches job requirements."[2]

Jill's concern about screening candidates using smart tech dovetails with concerns we have previously raised about embedded bias. Hiring discrimination against Black Americans has stayed steady for the last twenty-five years,[3] and males and white-sounding names are significantly more likely to get an interview than identical resumes with names that sound Asian, Black, Latinx, or female.[4] Without intentional inclusion and audits, tech can replicate or amplify bias; it can also mitigate discrimination. Tech can help advance those with the required skills versus a human preference for Ivy League schools, and nudge hiring managers to adjust their job criteria to engage a larger qualified pool by, for example, seeking a Masters degree or an MBA or adjusting for required years of experience.

However, Finlayson also notes that AI has the potential to anonymize applications and enable people to be found based on having the skills to do the job. Finlayson warns hiring managers, "If we don't control for biased criteria and data sets, AI will detect patterns and may replicate or amplify bias in our organizations." It is also important to note that if organizations continue using the same social and professional networks to post job openings and recruit new staff, they are also creating bias in the applicant pool even before smart tech is applied.

Automating first interviews is another area that smart tech tools can help automate. Structured interviews are far better in reducing bias than unstructured interviews. Smart tech can automate this consistency and ensure that every candidate has the opportunity to answer the same questions.[5] Smart Tech also offers convenience and efficiency for scheduling those interviews.

Some automated systems administer tests for skills or gaming systems that can help validate skills, which opens up application pools beyond degrees and years of experience. Others include personality assessment tests.

Finlayson warns that these systems may not be equitable because they lack independent auditing for equity. They are black boxes that make it difficult to understand who is being screened out and how the scores are calculated. Most controversial is the use of facial recognition software to assess a candidate's potential and fit for a position. This is how people make judgments in hiring. However, having a black box bot interpret a candidate's "intonation," "inflection," and "emotions" to determine social intelligence (interpersonal skills), communication skills, personality traits, and overall job aptitude doesn't feel human-centered. Gaming systems used to assist in hiring also create barriers for older workers, non-native English speakers, and others with personal (and preferably private) limitations.[6]

WORKPLACE WELL-BEING AND AUTOMATION

Healthy workplace culture is essential for employee well-being. Well-being includes several dimensions: physical health and safety, emotional health, financial stability, intellectual satisfaction, and having a sense of purpose.

When the workplace culture doesn't adequately support these aspects of employee well-being, the result is often stress and burnout. The World Health Organization (WHO) recently focused attention on the problem of work-related stress, updating its definition of workplace burnout as an "occupational phenomenon."

According to WHO, burnout is characterized by "feelings of energy depletion or exhaustion; increased mental distance from one's job, or feelings of negativism or cynicism related to one's job; and reduced professional efficacy."[7,8] Sounds like working for a non-profit, right?

Of course, organizations are not just being miserly when they create stressful environments. They are being squeezed by government and philanthropic funders unwilling to fully support the full cost of doing business. However, even if leaders are not able to pay staff as much as they would make in the commercial sector, it isn't an excuse to assume people should regularly work 60–80-hour weeks or constantly lurch from crisis to crisis. Sadly, this is the default setting for far too many organizations, particularly social service agencies. This is a long-standing trend that has recently been exposed and unfortunately exacerbated by the COVID-19 pandemic.

Chronic stress gradually erodes people's well-being, health, and relationships. In addition to an intimidating pile of work that nonprofit professionals undertake every day, there is a steady stream of clients whose lives often literally depend on the staff's efforts and the organization's programs. This kind of "urgent dependency" can contribute to a culture of scarcity and self-sacrifice.

Of course, agencies working in areas such as domestic violence and suicide prevention are going to have crises with clients for which staff people need to be available to respond. It is the made-up internal crisis with consequent sucking of time that makes work overwhelming and enervating for so many people. It is the paralyzing fear of risk taking that requires endless checking of staff work and enormous amounts of time spent reviewing what could go wrong instead of what could go right, the need to relitigate decisions after they've been made, and the constant fire drills that give people little control of their work.

Improving Well-Being

Organizations can address burnout by strengthening a sense of community at work, strong social relationships, a collegial environment, a workload that's not too burdensome, a sense of purpose at work, and a healthy work-life balance. Actively managing these kinds of activities is often referred to as people operations (people ops).

Integrating automation into the workplace has many benefits that can contribute to employee well-being, for example, not having to work excessive hours in completing repetitive, manual tasks. However, there is also the potential for automation to accelerate burnout and disrupt work-life balance if automation is allowed to overschedule people. Smart tech and automation can create space for nonprofit staff to create a healthy work-life balance, although some organizational leaders will consider it time to get more stuff done. As smart tech becomes increasingly prevalent in the workplace, workforce well-being also needs to be front and center. Leadership is required to use smart tech in ways that treat people well.

"It's a question of steering ourselves toward a future in which automation augments our work lives rather than . . . transforms the workplace into a surveillance panopticon," Rob Reich of Stanford University Human-Centered Artificial Intelligence Lab says. This means that when we integrate automation tools into the workplace, we need a wider range of values beyond the desire to increase efficiency. We need to be careful to avoid the risks that are inherent in bossware and instead use a framework that will help us make the best decisions for our organizations, people, and clients.

Bossware

"Bossware" is a type of smart tech that has the potential to undermine worker health and well-being. It includes cameras that automatically track employees' attention to software monitoring whether employees are off task. The pandemic hastened the adoption of tools to monitor employees remotely, generally without any discussion and debate with staff.

"The first key to addressing the bossware problem is awareness," Reich says. "The introduction of bossware should be seen as something that's done through a consensual practice, rather than at the discretion of the employer alone." Beyond awareness, researchers and policymakers need to get a handle on the ways employers use bossware to shift some of their business risks to their employees. For example, employers have historically borne the risk of inefficiencies such as paying staff during shifts when there are few customers. By using automated AI-based scheduling practices that assign work shifts based on demand, employers save money but essentially shift their risk to workers who can no longer expect a predictable or reliable schedule.

Reich is also concerned that bossware threatens privacy and can undermine human dignity. He asks, "Do we want to have a workplace in which employers know exactly how long we leave our desks to use the restroom, or an experience of work in which sending a personal email on your work computer is keystroke logged and deducted from your hourly pay, or in which your performance evaluations are dependent upon your maximal time on task with no sense of trust or collaboration?"

The Partnership for AI's Framework

The Partnership on AI's "Framework for Promoting Workforce Well-being in the AI-Integrated Workplace"[9] offers a set of guidelines for employers, workers, and other stakeholders to focus on employee well-being throughout the process of introducing automation into the workplace.[10,11] Some guidelines that are especially relevant for nonprofits that cover the intersection of automation and well-being include:

- *Physical Health:* Smart tech can support physical safety and health by monitoring environmental factors, tracking worker health indicators, building comprehensive pictures of risks, altering job profiles and ways of working that improve physical health, and nudging workers to healthy habits and behaviors: for example, helping encourage work-life boundaries and avoiding overworking or nudging employees to move and take screen and stretch breaks.

- *Financial Well-Being:* Smart Tech can support financial well-being through creation of new jobs, a redistribution of working time, and increased wages.

- *Intellectual Well-Being:* Smart Tech can support intellectual well-being through the creation of more job profiles that support non-routine and cognitive work for workers to pursue if they desire to. The need for new skills that comes with AI can provide learning opportunities for workers and increase workers' knowledge base.

- *Emotional Well-Being:* Smart tech can support emotional well-being through enabling stress-reducing forms of work, such as flexible work hours and location, and can reduce human bias and ensure inclusivity.

- *Purpose and Meaning:* Smart tech can support individuals in finding purpose and meaning at work through collaboration and by augmenting human capabilities so that larger personal and societal goals can be reached and challenges can be overcome.

Financial Management

Crunch time happens before every board meeting. The financial staff is frantically preparing reports to provide real-time analysis of the financial condition of the organization. Year-to-date budget reports require hours of reconciling the accounts with the correct accounting codes and cross-referencing statements and receipts. This level of precision coupled with the pressure of crunch time often results in mistakes.

Smart tech can help manage budgets and raise red flags regarding fraud and irregularities in real time, at a fraction of the time and cost of a person. Accurate accounts enable organizations to become more sophisticated, and accurate financial forecasters mean more accurate forecasting.[12]

Another application called ExpenseIt can scan and automatically assign accounting codes to receipts. This saves an enormous amount of time preparing financial reports for funders, regulatory agencies, and the IRS.

Some systems also incorporate chatbots to answer questions from staff or donors such as, "What percentage of our annual fundraising campaign goal have we met?" or "Is my contribution tax-deductible?"[13]

Automation makes human oversight of accounting systems more important than ever. If there are irregularities in the use of, say, an ATM card, a manager needs to get involved very quickly to untangle the situation. In addition, your organization should never want a staff person interfacing with a chatbot to discuss why they need an advance on their paycheck.

People need to stay in charge of asking mission-critical questions such as: Are your financial predictions and budget decisions reinforcing implicit biases? Are your core organizational values and principles driving finance, or is it the other way around? Ronald Tompkins of 82nd Street Academics noted, "Accounting software will perform oversight and hindsight while the human accountant provides insight and foresight."[14]

World Learning, an international nonprofit organization, automated its financial function in stages. First it moved its accounting to the cloud, and then it integrated its financial data with its program data to create a comprehensive data system accessible by staff around the globe for real-time decision-making.[15]

IMPROVING ORGANIZATION-WIDE WORKFLOW

Workflow bottlenecks are enormous sources of inefficiency and frustration for staff. Not many nonprofits have the resources to hire administrative assistants to schedule meetings, answer questions, track project deadlines, and other tasks. The busyness of organizations also makes it more likely that departments will be cut off from one another, making it difficult to know what is happening within other departments, much less get questions answered. Smart tech can help with all of these problems.[16]

Scheduling and Updates

Virtual-assistant bots can schedule meetings without the back and forth that even a tool like Doodle involves. But that's just the beginning of what a smart assistant such as Siri, Google Assistant, Slackbot, and Cortana can do. They can drive a process of reflection and continuous improvement that can lead to both small and large breakthroughs. These activities may include regularly cruising through files, correspondence, and calendars to look for bottlenecks to processes. Virtual assistants can also create and send a message summarizing the status of projects to team members by asking key questions such as: "What did I do yesterday?" "What am I doing today?" "What's blocking me?" The answers to these questions can inform weekly status meetings of the team.[17]

Busting Silos

Internal data silos are enormous barriers for organizational effectiveness. It can be difficult to raise money when fundraisers aren't aware of programmatic outcomes. It is enormously helpful for the finance department not just to know how much money is spent on programs but how and why. Bots can break down barriers and improve collaboration across the organizational departments, paving the way for innovations.

Oxfam is an international nonprofit working in 90 countries with more than 10,000 employees. It faced a challenge most international organizations do of balancing the need for central control while encouraging local innovation. Without an overarching way of managing communications and learning, the organization had become balkanized.

Oxfam turned to smart tech to solve the problem of communication among Oxfam affiliates around the world that was limited to email and information and insights spread among thousands of files on internal drives. OxBot is a jargon-busting bot that will tell employees what specific acronyms mean. It also provides a link to other internal sources of information to find out more. Smart tech searches through internal files looking for patterns and insights of successful approaches to internal and external problems. For larger organizations with lots of documents or even a smaller organization with an internal drive that is messier than a kitchen sink, it saves an enormous amount of time for a bot to search through files and files to find the information you need.[18]

EDITING, CUSTOMIZING, AND REVIEWING CONTENT

Human language has many levels at which it can be analyzed and processed: from characters and individual words through grammatical structures and sentences, even paragraphs or full texts. Google's Gmail uses smart tech to make suggestions for emails. Your phone autocorrects text messages. Grammarly is an example of an AI grammar checker that can tell you if you used an Oxford comma correctly and just like a human copy editor mark up your text.

Inclusivity is an app created by George Weiner at Whole Whale to read and analyze website text and highlight language that isn't inclusive.[19,20] The bot crawls through a page, compares the language on a site against Whole Whale's database of inclusive language, and makes recommendations.

There are other apps aimed at making communications more persuasive. Crystal is an app with an algorithm called "Personality AI," which analyzes online data points to accurately identify a person's motivations, communication style, and other behavioral traits. The software integrates with other sales and marketing AI-driven platforms including Salesforce and Hubspot.

PROJECT MANAGEMENT

Project management takes up an enormous amount of time and effort within organizations. It includes scheduling, monitoring progress against goals, assigning tasks to staff, and communications with stakeholders. This typically is done manually by constantly updating spreadsheets and documents. There are smart tech project management tools to reduce the workload of project managers.[21,22] There are mainly two types of tools:

- *Project Scheduling Software:* This helps in planning, tracking, and analyzing projects. Examples include Trello and Asana.

- *Resource Scheduling Software:* This helps allocate resources like equipment rooms, staff, and other resources. Examples include Smith.AI and Calendly.[23]

CONCLUSION

Nonprofits operate on shoestring budgets with limited staffing. Why tie up valuable staff time doing repetitive, boring, soul-sucking, time-consuming administrative tasks when available smart tech tools can do the work of ten interns? Smart tech in the back office is bound to return a huge dividend of time to nonprofits.

ENDNOTES

1. Mercer's 2019 Global Talent Trends study identifies four top trends shaping the future of work (February 26, 2019), https://www.mercer.com/newsroom/with-more-business-disruption-expected-making-organizations-future-fit-is-top-of-mind-new-study-finds.html.
2. Author interview with Jill Finlayson, July 10, 2021.
3. Lincoln Quillian, Devah Pager, Arnfinn H. Midtbøen, and Ole Hexel, "Hiring Discrimination Against Black Americans Hasn't Declined in 25 Years," *Harvard Business Review* (October 11, 2017),

https://hbr.org/2017/10/hiring-discrimination-against-black-americans-hasnt-declined-in-25-years.

4. Dina Gerdeman, "Minorities Who 'Whiten' Job Resumes Get More Interviews," Harvard Business School, *Working Knowledge* (May 17, 2017), https://hbswk.hbs.edu/item/minorities-who-whiten-job-resumes-get-more-interviews.

5. Author interview with Jill Finlayson, July 10, 2021.

6. Iris Bohnet, "How to Take the Bias Out of Interviews," *Harvard Business Review* (April 18, 2016), https://hbr.org/2016/04/how-to-take-the-bias-out-of-interviews.

7. World Health Organization, "Burn-out an 'occupational phenomenon': International Classification of Diseases" (28 May 2019), https://www.who.int/news/item/28-05-2019-burn-out-an-occupational-phenomenon-international-classification-of-diseases.

8. Rhitu Chatterjee and Carmel Wroth, "WHO Redefines Burnout as a 'Syndrome' Linked to Chronic Stress at Work," National Public Radio (May 28, 2019), https://www.npr.org/sections/health-shots/2019/05/28/727637944/who-redefines-burnout-as-a-syndrome-linked-to-chronic-stress-at-work.

9. Jonathan Timm, "The Plight of the Overworked Nonprofit Employee," *The Atlantic* (August 24, 2016), https://www.theatlantic.com/business/archive/2016/08/the-plight-of-the-overworked-nonprofit-employee/497081/.

10. Beth Kanter and Aliza Sherman, *The Happy, Healthy Nonprofit: Strategies for Impact without Burnout* (New York: Wiley, 2016).

11. Katharine Miller, "Future of Work: Beyond Bossware and Job-Killing Robots," Stanford University Human-Centered Artificial Intelligence Center (July 6, 2021), https://hai.stanford.edu/news/future-work-beyond-bossware-and-job-killing-robots.

12. Katharine Miller, "Future of Work: Beyond Bossware and Job-Killing Robots," Stanford University Human-Centered Artificial Intelligence Center (July 6, 2021), https://hai.stanford.edu/news/future-work-beyond-bossware-and-job-killing-robots.

13. Katharine Miller, "Future of Work: Beyond Bossware and Job-Killing Robots," Stanford University Human-Centered Artificial Intelligence Center (July 6, 2021), https://hai.stanford.edu/news/future-work-beyond-bossware-and-job-killing-robots.

14. Pai Staff, "Framework for Promoting Workforce Well-being in the AI-Integrated Workplace," Partnership for AI (August 27, 2020), https://www.partnershiponai.org/workforce-wellbeing/).

15. Shivani Govil, "Voices: What AI Does for Accountants," *Accounting Today* (January 27, 2020), https://www.accountingtoday.com/opinion/what-ai-does-for-accountants.

16. Phil Goldstein, "How Nonprofits Can Effectively Use AI Tools," *BizTech* (April 9, 2019), https://biztechmagazine.com/article/2019/04/how-nonprofits-can-effectively-use-ai-tools.

17. Forbes Nonprofit Council, "How Will Automation and AI Change the Nonprofit World?" *Forbes Magazine* (April 4, 2019), https://www.forbes.com/sites/forbesnonprofitcouncil/2019/04/04/how-will-automation-and-ai-change-the-nonprofit-world/.

18. Laura Stanley, "How charities can reclaim a day with automation," Charity Digital (July 29, 2021), https://charitydigital.org.uk/topics/how-charities-can-reclaim-a-day-with-automation-9046.

19. Shreeya Chourasia, "Best AI Assistant of 2021," TRO (August 5, 2021), https://techresearchonline.com/blog/best-ai-assistant-of-2021/#.

20. Inclusivity Crawler, Whole Whale, https://inclusivity.wholewhale.com.

21. Facebook Workplace, "Oxfam: Using Custom Integrations to Revolutionize Work," August 28, 2021, https://www.workplace.com/case-studies/oxfam.

22. "Top 8 AI-Powered Project Management Tools To Use in 2021," *Analytics India* (May 5, 2021), https://analyticsindiamag.com/top-8-ai-powered-project-management-tools-to-use-in-2021/.

23. Shreeya Chourasia, "Best AI Assistant of 2021," TRO (August 5, 2021), https://techresearchonline.com/blog/best-ai-assistant-of-2021/#.

CHAPTER **11**

Smart Philanthropy

INTRODUCTION

People give to charity for many different reasons: admiration for particular leaders or institutions, outrage at injustice, empathy for people who are suffering, passion for culture, religious conviction, gratitude and a desire to give back, or countless other reasons. Giving can be a spontaneous reaction to misfortune like a natural disaster, or it can be very strategically done over a long period of time. Strategic donors give with intention: they set objectives based on their interests; do their homework to identify the most effective organizations addressing a problem in a geographic location; and consider such variables as giving models and legal considerations. Smart tech is helping donors be more strategic in their giving choices.

In this chapter, we will explore the ways smart tech is being used to create customized experiences for donors at every level. We will also outline ways major donors should be investing in the ethical and responsible use of smart tech. Finally, we will discuss the need for large-scale investments in program evaluation to create great outcomes data to be used to feed smart tech systems.

AUTOMATING DONOR ADVISING

Effective philanthropy is a delicate balance between emotional and intellectual needs and interests of donors.[1]

We want stories and local impact (heart), and we want strategic plans and data on results (head). Smart tech is going to help inform and shape all of these aspects. Smart tech for philanthropy will help:

- Create funding plans that match their personal interests.

- Identify the most pressing needs within social impact areas or geographic locations.

- Find effective nonprofits working to address those needs.

- Learn more about giving models, tax implications, legal considerations, and so on.

This is not an easy task. Dean Karlan, a leading economic expert on program evaluation, said, "We lack good metrics and analysis on the impact of charities that then can be lined up with donor preferences for causes. And we lack a broad market driven by impact data, a market environment which could lead to more everyday donors supporting high-impact charities."[2]

Rhodri Davies, former head of policy at Charities Aid Foundation (CAF), coined the term "philgorithm"[3] to describe the use of algorithms to direct philanthropic giving. According to Davies, "If we could use machine learning to analyze data both on need and on the social impact of nonprofits and other interventions, it would enable identification of where the most pressing needs were at any given time, as well as the most effective ways of addressing those needs through philanthropy."[4]

Digital platforms matching donors with causes are not new. What is new is the ability of platforms to match donors and causes based on the specific interests of donors, and keep them informed about the impact their gift is making in real time.

Philanthropy Cloud was originally developed as Salesforce .org's internal employee giving tool. It is now available as an employee engagement product for corporations to facilitate employee volunteering, giving, and other social impact activities. Nick Bailey, the Salesforce general manager of Philanthropy Cloud, notes, "It [the algorithm] can help employees find and connect with the causes they're passionate about. It allows us to do personalized philanthropy at scale."[5]

Smart tech is very good—and fast—at this kind of task. According to Bailey, "The user can tell the application where they are geographically, the causes they care about, the skills they have and combined with the actions they take in the app, the algorithm serves up the right opportunity to engage them at the right time."[6]

Deluxe, a 105-year-old company that actually created the checkbook, became a Philanthropy Cloud client in 2020, just as the pandemic and protests over racial injustice started to erupt. The company implemented eight different campaigns that raised a total of $260,000 from employees. According to Alexandra Goodwin, senior foundation relations partner at Deluxe Foundation, Philanthropy Cloud created more transparency and visibility about employees' philanthropic and volunteer interests: "With over 6,000 employees across the US and Canada, the data generated by the platform allowed us to understand trends and other insights about our employees' community engagement efforts. Through the system, employees can also share photos and feedback on their experiences that are available to other employees. This helps employees feel connected to one another around a common goal of giving. The data generated from an automated system helps us improve the foundation's impact we're making with donations and volunteering and employee engagement."[7]

Candid, a leading source of information on nonprofit and philanthropic efforts, has been manually coding and labeling data for use by smart tech for years. Candid's Vice President of Products Jake Garcia notes, "Now that we have enough data in the system that has been accurately categorized, nonprofits (and program officers) can do queries such as 'What nonprofits are working on clean water projects and are based in New York and build wells in Ethiopia?'"[8,9]

Candid's data is based on tax return data that takes two years for the IRS to process and release. To address this issue, Candid has built a news media monitoring platform to provide real-time data on giving. It scrapes about 300,000 news articles on philanthropy per day from the web and categorizes them by subject, population group, and locations. The algorithm determines the most frequently mentioned organizations and geographic areas, or the establishment of new giving programs or grants.

DonorsChoose matches donors with teachers in need of basic supplies and other kinds of help. After several years of effort to prepare their data for smart tech, they were able to build a machine learning algorithm that predicts in which of 12 categories a teacher-requested item fails. It automatically categorizes classroom projects so that both partner organizations and donors can easily find the resources they wish to fund.[10]

Another approach to smart tech for philanthropy is the advent of "robo advisors," chatbots available to donors at any level that provide advice on charitable giving to their menus of other financial investment and savings options.

Smart tech is becoming an essential benefit for matching donors and causes. The field of smart tech for social good, though, also needs philanthropic investments.

PHILANTHROPIC INVESTMENT IN THE USE OF SMART TECH FOR SOCIAL GOOD

Just as nonprofits have a responsibility to use smart tech sparingly and well, so too do philanthropic organizations. Leading developers in the use of smart tech for social good Ben Brockman, Skye Hersh, Brigitte Hoyer Gosselink, Florian Maganza, and Micah Berman outlined criteria for supporting smart tech projects.[11] These include:

Size of potential impact. What is the breadth of a solution or set of solutions—how many people can it help? What is the depth? For example, does it modestly increase beneficiaries' income or save a life?

Implementation feasibility. Is it possible to build an algorithm of sufficient accuracy that outperforms the status-quo, non-AI option? What is the differential impact of AI compared to other approaches to solve this problem? Is high-quality data necessary for building the algorithm available or can it be obtained?

Opportunity area synergies. Are there many different entities currently working on similar problems? Are there fixed, catalytic investments that would have a nonlinear impact in enabling various other AI for good interventions? Is there a preeminent organization that could build and deploy initial solutions at scale in partnership with a funder?

Programmatic areas ripe for investment in the use of smart tech are medical diagnostic tools, communication support for marginalized communities and languages, and agricultural yield prediction.

Philanthropy also needs to invest in the capacity of individual nonprofit organizations to use smart tech well. A couple of areas for investment that could have a catalytic effect for the field are nonprofit data collaboratives and program evaluation.

Nonprofit Data Collaboratives

A great way to positively influence an entire field is to invest in a nonprofit data collaborative, as we described in Chapter 5, "Data, Data, Data." Most organizations won't have the resources to hire their own data scientists. Nonprofit data collaboratives will make it more likely that there is full transparency for the use of the data. It also removes commercial companies from the opportunity to obfuscate or sell the data. A philanthropist could invest in, say, a data collaborative on hunger in Cincinnati to understand where and how hunger manifests itself in the city and where and how giving will have the greatest impact.

Vilas S. Dhar and Kay Firth-Butterfield write, "Philanthropic organizations should play a central role in supporting efforts to make data more accessible to grantees through vehicles such as data cooperatives and data trusts. These entities link data held by otherwise separate groups, providing even small nonprofits with robust data and analysis capabilities."[12] Dhar and Butterfield point out that philanthropic organizations also address privacy concerns by making the data confidential and applied only for its intended use—different from commercial data brokers.

Investing in Program Evaluation

The best way to have a positive impact on social change is to invest in program evaluation to create quality results data needed to power smart tech. However, there is one enormous caveat about program evaluation in the autonomous world: program evaluation data is *not* the same data generated by digital tech we have been discussing throughout this book. We need to dig into this important issue further.

Adding to the lack of quality data about outcomes is the growing confusion between data needed for program evaluation and the data smart tech needs and generates. These are entirely different fields with fundamentally different purposes. Nonprofits create a theory of change for programs and services that connect the dots between what they plan to do and the outcomes or results. Some of the data is relatively straightforward, for example, the number of people who showed up for a program or bought a ticket to an event. Other data is much harder to define and collect. For instance, what effect did the program have on the people who showed up? How are they different or better and are these changes adding up to the kinds of results the organization is in the business of creating? Measuring these kinds of outcomes is where program evaluation becomes really hard and elusive. It is incredibly difficult to accurately predict because of all of the ways real life has a habit of interrupting perfect plans.

Digital data used to power smart tech—such as clicks, kinds of comments, subject of photos, content of forms, answers to chatbots, organizational data, and third-party data sets—is expensive and abundant. Data scientists swim through all of this data (we will call it big data) to find patterns and make predictions about what people will do or say or believe.

Data scientists focus on results for one person; evaluators focus on results for whole populations. Data scientists look for patterns to reinforce behavior; social scientists create theories to be proven in practice.

Peter York and Michael Bamberger point out that part of the problem is that traditional evaluators have been slow to embrace big data. This isn't surprising given that big data has been collected without their input, in another department, and for different purposes. We need to use big data to inform program evaluation efforts. For instance, big data can be used to gain insights on shifts of attitudes and behaviors at scale using technologies like chatbots.[13]

Finally, we need to evaluate the use and efficacy of smart tech for social good. The power and opacity of smart tech coupled with the possibility that smart tech could be used for unethical purposes (wittingly or not) deserves scrutiny. Questions that need to be asked and answered are:

- How is smart tech changing the interaction clients and constituents are having with organizations? Is this helping or hurting outcomes?

- Is smart tech exacerbating racial and gender inequities?

- What are the unintended consequences of using smart tech for social change?

CONCLUSION

Smart tech adds to the growing ecosystem of ways to give to causes. It can provide insights and intelligence to give strategically. However, the nonprofit sector needs philanthropy to invest in outcomes evaluation in order to have quality data on results to match the interests of donors.

ENDNOTES

1. Andrés Spokoiny, "What Prompts Us to Give? Balancing Head and Heart," *eJewish Philanthropy* (May 15, 2019) (https://ejewishphilanthropy.com/what-prompts-us-to-give-balancing-head-and-heart/).

2. Dean Karlin, "Which Charity Will Do the Most Good with Your Donation? This Simple Tool Can Tell You," Kellogg Insights (December 2, 2019), (https://insight.kellogg.northwestern.edu/article/nonprofits-most-impact-charitable-giving).

3. Rhodri Davies, "Automatic For The People: What Might A Philanthropy Algorithm Look Like?" CAFonline (November 17, 2017), https://www.cafonline.org/about-us/blog-home/giving-thought/the-future-of-doing-good/automatic-for-the-people-what-might-a-philanthropy-algorithm-look-like.

4. Author interview with Rhodri Davies, September 5, 2019, for "AI4Giving: Unlocking Generosity with Artificial Intelligence: The Future of Giving" by Beth Kanter and Allison Fine.

5. Author interview with Nick Bailey, August 5, 2019, for "AI4Giving: Unlocking Generosity with Artificial Intelligence: The Future of Giving" by Beth Kanter and Allison Fine.

6. Author interview with Nick Bailey, August 5, 2019, for "AI4Giving: Unlocking Generosity with Artificial Intelligence: The Future of Giving" by Beth Kanter and Allison Fine.

7. Author interview with Alexandra Goodwin, July 30, 2021.

8. Author interview with Nick Bailey, August 5, 2019, for "AI4Giving: Unlocking Generosity with Artificial Intelligence: The Future of Giving" by Beth Kanter and Allison Fine.

9. Candid Learning, "Funding Smarter: Using Candid Tools to Inform and Share Your Foundation's Work" (August 28, 2021), https://learning.candid.org/training/funding-smarter-using-candid-tools-to-inform-and-share-your-foundations-work/.

10. Author interview with Mohammad Radiyat, July 15, 2019, for "AI4Giving: Unlocking Generosity with Artificial Intelligence: The Future of Giving" by Beth Kanter and Allison Fine.

11. Ben Brockman, Skye Hersh, Brigitte Hoyer Gosselink, Florian Maganza, and Micah Berman, "Investing in AI for Good," *Stanford Social Innovation Review* (May 11, 2021), https://ssir.org/articles/entry/investing_in_ai_for_good.

12. Vilas S. Dhar and Kay Firth-Butterfield, "Philanthropy Needs to Prepare Itself for a World Powered by Artificial Intelligence," *Chronicle of Philanthropy* (March 30, 2021), https://www.philanthropy.com/article/philanthropy-needs-to-prepare-itself-for-a-world-powered-by-artificial-intelligence.

13. Peter York and Michael Bamberger, "Measuring Results and Impact in the Age of Big Data," Rockefeller Foundation (March, 2020), https://www.rockefellerfoundation.org/wp-content/uploads/Measuring-results-and-impact-in-the-age-of-big-data-by-York-and-Bamberger-March-2020.pdf.

PART III

WHERE WE GO FROM HERE

CHAPTER 12

A Smarter Future

INTRODUCTION

As we've outlined in this book, smart tech is quickly changing what we do and how we do it. Leadership is required to actively and purposefully create the conditions for people and organizations to thrive. The combination of leadership and smart tech creates the possibility of a very different kind of future. Here is our vision for organizations and society, a future powered by smart tech that is healthier, kinder, and more generous.

THE FUTURE OF NONPROFIT WORK

We imagine a future where nonprofits use smart tech well and reap the benefits of the dividend of time. This will allow smart organizations to usher in a new era of nonprofit organizations that don't specialize in burnout and scarcity. Here are ways we want to see nonprofits working as smart nonprofits:

- Clarify and honor the boundaries between work and home lives.

- Provide more time off. Maybe four-day workweeks are possible. Certainly more vacation time is warranted. And planned sabbaticals for staff at every level would be a huge and deserved benefit for long-serving staff.

181

- Focus on the real work, not the busyness. We want smart, talented people being creative, proactive problem solvers. We want organizations that nurture the talents of staff and support their growth and learning.

- We want staff to end their days with a greater sense of satisfaction that comes from really helping to heal the world, rather than feeling numb and exhausted.

The work of organizations will change. It will hopefully include:

- More time spent getting to know clients, board members, donors, and volunteers: learning who they are and what their needs are; solving problems before they turn into crises for clients; understanding why your cause is so important to board members, donors, and volunteers.

- Emphasis on solving rather than serving problems. We want more organizations to become great advocates for more money and support for, say, affordable housing, and spend less time turning away enormous numbers of people who need emergency housing.

- Real-time information on what's working and what isn't, what services are needed, who needs help, and how to get it to them.

A Better Path Forward

We need to do more than change the contours and practices of individual organizations. We need to reknit communities that never recovered from the atomizing effects of the precipitous drop in social capital at the beginning of the twenty-first century that resulted in the atomizing of citizens from one another and the loss of trust in and declining membership in institutions such as religious congregations, unions, and clubs. These communities are now reeling from the social and economic impact of COVID-19.

Nonprofits are the backbones of communities. We provide healthcare and emergency services and run schools and arts organizations. We need to take the lead on reknitting communities where people are known and cared for, where loneliness is reduced and social capital is increased. Nonprofits can help neighbors get to know one another and begin to rely on each other for help and information. Nonprofits can become beacons of ethical leadership by restoring people's faith and trust in institutions in general.

We can also create real-time information systems for people in need. There are already 2-1-1 systems people can call for emergency services. Smart tech could make these systems much more robust by using the data to predict future problems (e.g., increased need for food assistance and increased homelessness) and connecting donors to give for these needs in real time. For instance, Houston could have 36 homeless people in need of a bed on a Tuesday night. The smart system would not only direct social service agencies to send these people to beds that are available, but enable donors to give, say, $100 to house each person.[1]

Local municipalities and organizations should be active proponents of robot companions. The loneliness epidemic hits frail seniors the hardest. Most people want to stay in their homes as they age. Robot companions will be far less expensive than home health aides, for whom we already have a shortage. Robots will be able to provide basic healthcare, such as measuring blood pressure, preparing food, monitoring vital signs, and reading and talking to people. We would prefer people socializing with one another; however, robots are a good alternative.

Integrating causes into every aspect of our everyday lives will also help remake communities. There are apps to help us do everything imaginable, including exercise, shop, diet, and manage our money. Betterment is a money managing smart app. Users can pay bills, make investments, and donate to causes using the app. Users can access a dashboard to see all of their financial plans and transactions in one place and track savings and other goals. This is the direction of financial management: real-time data and dashboards to see all of your investments and accounts at once, including your charitable activities. An app like Betterment could also become a home base for lifestyles that incorporate philanthropy, green purchases, volunteer opportunities, investments in BIPOC-owned companies, basically any filter a person wants to make sure all of their financial transactions reflect their values and interests. There could even be scores for living your values. The app would provide updates and reminders of volunteer activities and the ability to remind friends as well.

SOCIETAL CHANGES

Finally, we need to address changes at the societal level to create more equitable communities. There are many societal concerns, including diversity in the programming field, data sovereignty, and civil rights.

Diversifying the Field of Programmers and Data Scientists

The field of programming continues to be dominated by white men, making unintentional bias baked into computer code more likely. Diversifying a field like programming is exactly the kind of problem the nonprofit sector specializes in solving. This won't be easy, of course. A recent report finds that diversity increases through STEM (science, technology, engineering, math) programs is stubborn, slow, and uneven. For instance, the study found that, "Black workers comprise just 5% in engineering and architecture jobs. There has been no change in the share of Black workers in STEM jobs since 2016."[2]

We need more funding for STEM programs and an increased awareness in tech companies and tech users of the impact that a lack of diversity has on embedded bias. We need to make the recruitment and training of diverse people as programmers and data scientists a top priority.

Data Sovereignty

One of the biggest economic questions to be addressed in the next several years is: Who owns personal data? This is not just an economic question; it is a profound moral one as well.

Researchers began to collect DNA samples from indigenous populations in the 1990s. The original purpose was to ensure that they preserved samples from vanishing tribes. The resulting data sets were made publicly available for science. What those original researchers couldn't have anticipated was that "science" would soon include companies like Ancestry and 23andMe that added the information to their databases from which they profit. In 2018, GlaxoSmithKline invested $300 million in 23andMe to use 23andMe's database of digital sequence information for its own research.[3] This is reminiscent of what happened to the cancer cells extracted without permission from Harriet Lacks in 1951. These durable and replicable HeLa cells became vital for fundamental research and drug development. It took decades and a best-selling book before Harriet's descendants were compensated for this gift to science.[4] There is a growing movement for data sovereignty by Indigenous people. The idea is that Indigenous people govern the collection, ownership, and application of their own data.[5]

There needs to be a growing movement for data sovereignty for all people. We need to change the default settings of having to opt out of data collection systems, to an opt-in system that every individual owns and regulates. There will be furious opposition to this change since the vast data-sucking machines are the fuel for the big data robber barons. However, just because vacuuming up personal data for corporate profit has become the norm doesn't make it smart or right.

We appreciate nonprofit resistance to changing these standards. User data has become essential intelligence for fundraising and program delivery operations. However, is it also possible organizations are afraid that users will opt out of data systems entirely? If that's true, if you can't make a solid, persuasive case to your clients, donors, and volunteers on why it is important to your efforts to collect data and that you are a reliable steward for its ethical use, perhaps you should think twice about doing it in the first place.

We do not have to follow commercial norms that default to "whatever we can get away with." There are ethical options for data sovereignty that begin with every person's right to own their personal data. In this new scenario, individuals give companies permission to use their data for clearly identified purposes and a limited amount of time.

Data sovereignty is not a new idea. Kaliya Hamlin, Doc Searls, Phil Windley, Kim Cameron and others have been advocating for personal data rights, what they call data identity, since the early 2000s. Their appeals have been subsumed by the avaricious interests of corporations. So far. Perhaps, like early suffragettes and civil rights warriors, they have laid the groundwork for the battles ahead.

We could even rent our data to companies or donate it to causes as microdonations. Rhodri Davies describes this idea. "The monetization of personal data through self-sovereign identity may . . . create huge new volumes of micro-transactions. We could harness this for charity by introducing mechanisms that direct a percentage of each transaction automatically to good causes . . . "[6]

A New Era in Civil Rights

Sonia Katyal, codirector of the Berkeley Center for Law and Technology predicted that in 2030, "Questions about privacy, speech, the right of assembly and technological construction of personhood will all re-emerge in this new AI context . . . Who will benefit and who will be disadvantaged in this new world depends on how broadly we analyze these questions today, for the future. " We believe that we need to wrestle with these questions now and not wait until embedded bias widens and deepens the racial, gender, and wealth gaps we already have.[7]

Who decides? The US Department of Defense is experimenting with the automation of lethal weapons for warfare. This means drones and robots will have the power to decide whether and when to kill enemy combatants. The technology is already available to make this possible. However, it raises a host of moral and ethical qualms. Civilians could easily be mistaken for enemy troops. When the cost of war is lower in human terms, it makes it more likely that decision makers will go to war. Most importantly, who will decide that autonomous killer drones are acceptable?[8]

Who is going to decide what the boundaries are for the use of smart tech to substitute for human decision-making? When will smart cars be safe to drive? What parameters will be created for robots providing home healthcare? Can they diagnose their clients? Can they provide drugs? Who is going to license and oversee these software and hardware entities?

William Uricchio, media scholar and professor of comparative media studies at MIT, commented, "AI and its related applications face three problems: development at the speed of Moore's Law, development in the hands of a technological and economic elite, and development without benefit of an informed or engaged public. The public is reduced to a collective of consumers awaiting the next technology."[9]

We cannot afford to be that passive group of consumers. We need to be an educated, active citizenry that presses elected officials and other decision makers on the future we want, with smart tech supporting us, not the other way around. Elected officials have so far shown very little interest in reining in big tech companies. Although there are bipartisan grumbles right now, there is little indication Congress will have the stomach (and willingness to forgo donations) to actually curtail their use in data extraction and invasions of privacy. Citizens are going to have to put the steel in the spines of elected officials and insist that the ethical use of smart tech cannot be left in the hands of corporations alone.

The public must insist on a future where smart tech companies are properly regulated and monitored to actively mitigate bias and unethical uses of their technology. This will require opening up black boxes so that we can see how they work, seeing what data they are using to train and use their systems, insisting on proof that the tools and systems aren't biased, and creating guidelines for the use of data with significant penalties for its misuse. The European Union already does this, and we can pursue a similar course.

This is where the nonprofit sector should be leading and not following. Our associations and membership groups should be working right now to set standards for our own use of smart tech that can become a model for other sectors. Perhaps there is a need and opportunity to create a good housekeeping seal for the ethical and responsible use of smart tech. Finally, we need to call out any uses of smart tech that degrade our common humanity. This includes strengthening workers' rights to be managed not by algorithms alone, and everyone's right to control our own data.

The future of civil rights is even going to include robots. We need to begin asking and answering questions such as: "At what point might a robot, algorithm, or other autonomous system be held accountable for the decisions it makes or the actions it initiates?" The reverse also holds true: "At what point, might humans be held accountable to robots?" We appreciate that these might sound like absurd arguments right now; however, the fundamental idea is very important: How are we going to assign moral responsibility for actions taken by autonomous tech?[10]

CONCLUSION

While no timetable exists for becoming a smart nonprofit, it is urgent that you and your organization begin the work today. The costs of willfully ignoring the impact of automation are unacceptable. All organizations are going to need to be curious, open, thoughtful, careful, and engaged about the use of smart tech. Today's complex and hard-to-solve problems require different solutions, and smart tech gives you the opportunity to reset cultural norms of busyness and transactions and become smarter and better and more successful.

The gift of time offers you, your colleagues, and constituents the opportunity to build stronger relationships, think of new approaches to do the work, and do the kind of soul-fulfilling work that initially interested you. If every nonprofit in the sector can transform itself into a smart nonprofit, we can transform the world.

ENDNOTES

1. Catherine Clifford, "Artificial Intelligence will generate enough wealth to pay each adult $13,500 a year," Cnbc.com (March 17, 2021), https://www.cnbc.com/2021/03/17/openais-altman-ai-will-make-wealth-to-pay-all-adults-13500-a-year.html.

2. Richard Fry, Brian Kennedy, and Cary Funk, "STEM Jobs See Uneven Progress in Increasing Gender, Racial and Ethnic Diversity," Pew Research Center (April 1, 2021), https://www.pewresearch.org/science/2021/04/01/stem-jobs-see-uneven-progress-in-increasing-gender-racial-and-ethnic-diversity/.

3. Sabrina Imbler, "Training the Next Generation of Indigenous Data Scientists," *New York Times* (June 29, 2021), https://www.nytimes.com/2021/06/29/science/indigenous-data-microbiome-science.html.

4. National Institute of Health, "HeLa Cells: A Lasting Contribution to Biomedical Research," August 30, 2021, https://osp.od.nih.gov/scientific-sharing/hela-cells-landing/.

5. Kalen Goodluck, "Indigenous data sovereignty shakes up research," *High Country News* (October 8, 2020), https://www.hcn.org/issues/52.11/indigenous-affairs-covid19-indigenous-data-sovereignty-shakes-up-research.

6. Rhodri Davies, "Knowing Me, Knowing You: Self-sovereign Digital Identity and the Future for Charities," CAF blog (July 27, 2017), https://www.cafonline.org/about-us/blog-home/giving-thought/the-future-of-doing-good/self-sovereign-digital-identity-and-the-future-of-charity).

7. Janna Anderson and Lee Rainie, "Artificial Intelligence and the Future of Humans," Pew Research Center (December 10, 2018), https://www.pewresearch.org/internet/2018/12/10/artificial-intelligence-and-the-future-of-humans/).

8. Will Knight, "The Pentagon Inches Toward Letting AI Control Weapons," *Wired Magazine* (May 10, 2021), https://www.wired.com/story/pentagon-inches-toward-letting-ai-control-weapons).

9. Janna Anderson and Lee Rainie, "Artificial Intelligence and the Future of Humans," Pew Research Center (December 10, 2018), https://www.pewresearch.org/internet/2018/12/10/artificial-intelligence-and-the-future-of-humans/).

10. David Gunkel, "2020: The Year of Robot Rights," *MIT Press Reader* (January 7, 2020), https://thereader.mitpress.mit.edu/2020-the-year-of-robot-rights/).

Glossary: The Vocabulary of Smart Tech

actively anti-biased: Consciously striving to mitigate against all forms of bias to engage, understand, and treat all people fairly and equally. This includes addressing embedded biases and bias in the use of smart tech.

AI dividend: See *dividend of time*.

AI for Good (AI4Good):   The extensive use of AI in support of humanitarian causes, particularly to address transnational humanitarian crises. The main players include large nonprofit organizations in partnership with universities, international development agencies, healthcare, and large tech companies.

algorithm: A series of computations that ranges from the most simple to the most complex. Machine learning uses an algorithm to process data and discover rules that are hidden in the data, which are then encoded in a model that can be used to make predictions on new data.

augmented intelligence: See *co-botting*.

bias: Systematically favoring one group over another. Common areas of bias include gender, race, LGBTQ+, ableism, ageism, religion, class, education, nationality, and more.

big data: The huge amount of data that is constantly being created, stored, shared, used, and reviewed by machines to track, analyze, and make predictions about people's behavior.

busyness paradox: The state of being so busy concentrating on immediate, low-value tasks that a person's attention and ability to focus narrows, making it difficult to distinguish true crises from everyday work and to address important, mission-critical tasks. It often is accompanied by exhaustion, mistakes, and burnout.

co-botting: Humans and smart tech working together to improve productivity by balancing AI's speed and computing power with people's creativity, teamwork, and leadership. With proper planning, smart tech can augment and transform human roles without replacing them.

conversational smart tech: This includes chatbots, intelligent agents, and voice-activated helpers such as Facebook Messenger Bots, Siri, and Alexa. They employ natural language processing, machine learning and artificial intelligence.

data: Collections of information that can be structured into categories or unstructured like conversations. Data can be text, numbers, and images.

Data for Good (Data4Good): This burgeoning field is a subset of AI for Good (AI4Good). Data scientists, entrepreneurs, activists, and others use data science for social good, addressing extreme poverty, disease, and more.

data science: This is the emerging field of analyzing big data. Data scientists use their technological and social science skills to manage data, find trends, and develop actionable strategy. They employ industry knowledge, contextual understanding, and skepticism of existing assumptions.

data sovereignty: The concept of ownership of data, often considered from the perspective of data self-sovereignty, where people own their own data.

deep learning: Deep learning is a subset of machine learning that has networks capable of learning unsupervised from data that is unstructured or unlabeled. It uses multiple layers of artificial neurons to create a network that can make a decision based on raw input. Applications of deep learning include computer vision and speech recognition.

dividend of time: The time that is freed up for people and organizations as smart tech takes over hours of time-consuming rote tasks.

embedded bias: Bias that is built into a system and skews it. People are often unaware of this bias, making it difficult to specifically test for it and mitigate its effects.

first-party data: This is your own data. The term typically applies to a person, but it can also apply to an organization.

general smart tech: Artificial general intelligence (AGI) is the intelligence of a machine that has the capacity to understand or learn any intellectual task that a human being can. It does not exist yet, although there are active experiments and research being carried out to obtain general smart tech.

machine learning: Process and understand large volumes of data to identify patterns and make predictions or automate processes.

Moore's law: The 1965 prediction by Gordon E. Moore, founder of computer chip manufacturing company Intel, that the computational power of a single computer chip would double every two years. This prediction came true, and it changed the world.

narrow smart tech: Focuses on a specific type of artificial intelligence in which a technology outperforms humans in some very narrowly defined task. This includes machine learning and natural-language programming and what is mostly in everyday use today.

natural language processing (NLP): Process, decipher, understand, and generate human language in text or voice. NLP can perform sentiment analysis (positive or negative) and theme or content analysis. It can be combined with machine learning.

neural networks: Neural networks are a set of algorithms, modeled loosely after the human brain, that are designed to recognize patterns. They interpret data through a kind of machine perception by labeling or clustering raw data.

owned data sets: Data that an organization already owns and that has been collected in its databases on donors, stakeholders, finances, and other areas of operation.

people operations (people ops):   Actively managing aspects of the workplace such as the sense of community, social relationships, a collegial environment, a reasonable workload, a sense of purpose, a healthy work-life balance, and other factors, which can sometimes overlap with human resource functions as well.

reputation capital: A new form of capital created by big data that gauges people's reputation as citizens. China uses it to measure the behavior of citizens to create a society wherein "keeping trust is glorious and breaking trust is disgraceful."

second-party data: This is data created through collaboration with other organizations. The three typical approaches to using second-party data are open data sets, data collaboratives, and crowdsourcing data.

smart tech: This is an umbrella term for advanced digital technologies that make decisions *for* people, *instead* of people. It includes artificial intelligence (AI) and its subsets and cousins such as machine learning, natural language processing, smart forms, and chatbots.

super smart tech: Super artificial intelligence is the intelligence of machine that is more powerful and sophisticated than a human brain and can surpass human intelligence. It is beyond our current technological frontier and often portrayed in science fiction movies. Elon Musk suggests that smart tech has the potential to destroy human civilization, but many experts agree that we are decades away from having robot overlords.

supervised learning: A human categorizes the data by tagging it with keywords that will be important for the algorithm to use.

surveillance capitalism: The industry that tracks people's thoughts, conversations, movements, photos, and videos to create enormous stores of data about the habits, activities, and proclivities of individuals that can be used to track them online and on land.

third-party data sets: Data sets that are purchased or available through partnerships with companies and government or open-sourced or shared through data governance structures such as data trusts and collectives. The IRS Form 990 data is an example of a publicly available nonprofit data set. Giving Tuesday data collaborative and Fundraising Effectiveness Project (FEP) are examples of data trusts.

threat modeling: This is a risk-based planning approach used in the cyber-security field that can also be applied to ensure the safe and secure use of smart tech. It entails envisioning what could go wrong in a project, what data could be compromised, what system could be hacked, and what user could be harmed.

unstructured data: Huge amounts of data organized by theme and sentiment to help guide communication decision-making. It is collected and analyzed by natural language programming to learn and understand information, often about people and organizations.

unsupervised learning: Unsupervised learning is a type of machine learning algorithm used to draw inferences from data sets consisting of input data without labeled responses.

RESOURCES/BIBLIOGRAPHY

BOOKS

Benjamin, Ruha, *Race After Technology* (New York: Wiley, 2019).

Bernholz, Lucy, *How We Give Now: A Philanthropic Guide for the Rest of Us* (Cambridge: The MIT Press, 2021).

Bostrom, Nick, *Superintelligence: Paths, Dangers, Strategies* (United Kingdom: Oxford University Press, 2014).

Carr, Nicholas, *The Glass Cage* (New York: W. W. Norton & Company, 2015).

Carr, Nicholas, *The Shallows: What the Internet Is Doing to Our Brains*, (New York: W. W. Norton & Company, 2010).

Eubanks, Virginia, *Automating Inequality: How High-Tech Tools Profile, Police and Punish the Poor* (New York: St. Martin's Press, 2017).

Igo, Sarah E., *The Known Citizen: A History of Privacy in Modern America* (Cambridge: Harvard University Press, 2018).

Juma, Calestous, *Innovation and Its Enemies: Why People Resist New Technologies*, (Oxford: Oxford University Press, 2016).

Kanter, Beth, and Sherman, Aliza, *The Happy, Healthy Nonprofit: Strategies for Impact without Burnout* (New York: Wiley, October, 2016).

Lanier, Jaron, *You Are Not a Gadget: A Manifesto* (New York: First Vintage Books, 2010).

O'Neil, Cathy, *Weapons of Math Destruction: How Big Data Increases Inequality and Threatens Democracy* (New York: Penguin Random House, 2016).

Scott, Kevin, *Reprogramming The American Dream: From Rural America to Silicon Valley—Making AI Serve Us* (New York: HarperCollins, 2020).

Shirky, Clay, *Here Comes Everybody: The Power of Organizing Without Organizations* (New York: Penguin Group, 2009).

Shattuck, Steven, *Robots Make Bad Fundraisers: How Nonprofits Can Maintain the Heart in the Digital Age* (Bold & Bright Media, 2020).

Webb, Amy, *The Signals Are Talking: Why Today's Fringe Is Tomorrow's Mainstream* (New York: Public Affairs Publishing, 2016).

RESEARCH REPORTS, TOOLKITS, AND USEFUL WEBSITES

AI Adoption and Challenges

- **2020 State of Artificial Intelligence in the Nonprofit Sector Report**

  https://neonone.com/resources/guide/2020-sains-report/

  Annual research study of nonprofit and artificial intelligence adoption trends based on a survey of nonprofits.

- **NTEN: Equity Guide for Nonprofit Technology**

  https://www.nten.org/equity-guide-for-nonprofit-technology/

  Covers all nonprofit technology decision-making, including specific recommendations for data and algorithms. NTEN also covers an annual nonprofit technology conference that includes sessions on smart technology.

- **NetHope: AI Ethics Toolkit**

  https://solutionscenter.nethope.org/artificial-intelligence-ethics-for-nonprofits-toolkit

  Complete toolkit to help develop an ethical and responsible use of artificial intelligence and includes guidelines, case studies, and checklists. NetHope regularly hosts webinars and publishes blog posts and other resources on the topic.

- **Algorithmic Justice League**

  https://www.ajl.org/

  Organization's mission is to raise public awareness about the impacts of AI, equip advocates with empirical research to bolster campaigns, build the voice and choice of most impacted communities, and galvanize researchers, policymakers, and industry practitioners to mitigate AI biases and harms.

- **Pathways Through the Portal**

  http://emtechpathways.org/

  Civic Hall, with the generous support of the McGovern Foundation, gathered a group of researchers, technologists, and community organizers to explore the potential for emerging technologies to serve the public interest. For the purposes of this study, we used "emerging technologies" as a broad umbrella term (abbreviated as "EmTech" throughout). We paid special attention to public interest uses of artificial intelligence (AI), in particular machine learning (ML), natural language processing (NLP), automated decision support systems (ADSs), and bots, as well as to other tools including augmented and virtual reality (AR/VR), drones, remote sensing, and satellite imagery.

Fundraising and Philanthropy

- **AI4Giving: Unlocking Generosity with Artificial Intelligence by Beth Kanter and Allison Fine**

  http://www.ai4giving.org

  Funded by the Bill & Melinda Gates Foundation, this research paper is a landscape of analysis of giving and fundraising and artificial intelligence.

- **Machine-Made Goods: Artificial Intelligence in Giving and Philanthropy by Charity Aid Foundation**

  https://www.cafonline.org/about-us/caf-campaigns/campaigning-for-a-giving-world/future-good/machine-made-goods-charities-philanthropy-artificial-intelligence/machine-made-goods-impact-on-organisations-funding

  Overview of the current use of AI and the potential in the charity sector from Charity Aid Foundation in the UK.

- **Venture into the Future of Giving by _Economist Intelligence_**

    https://drive.google.com/file/d/1tHbUWjYs9i3 ZSqFiKKgWHzfQS_ZcLTOc/view

    Paper commissioned by the Gates Foundation that looks at a wide range of emerging technology, including artificial intelligence and the potential impact on philanthropy.

- **State of Artificial Intelligence in Advancement/Major Donors**

    https://gravyty.s3.amazonaws.com/2019aaacstateofaiina dvancement.pdf

    Survey of adoption for major gift officers from Gravyty.

- **Unlocking Real-Time Evidence for Practitioners: How Evaluation and Data Analytics Are Generating On-Demand, Actionable Evidence for Front-Line Practitioners at First Place for Youth and Gemma Services by Peter York, BCT Partners, July 2021**

    https://static1.squarespace.com/static/58d9ba1f 20099e0a03a3891d/t/61000cc42b91eb1daf990a27/ 1627393227147/FPFY-Gemma+Actionable+Evidence+Case+ Study+July21.pdf

    Case studies of nonprofit using machine learning for evaluation.

Data

- **Build It Back Better Report: Data for Good Stakeholders and Organizations**

    https://nationswell.com/tools/

    Build It Back Better initiative that focuses on how data and AI can drive positive innovation and change.

- **Data.Org**

  http://www.data.org

  Data.org is a platform for partnerships to build the field of data science for social impact.

AI4Good

- **Applying Artificial Intelligence for Social Good**

  https://www.mckinsey.com/featured-insights/artificial-intelligence/applying-artificial-intelligence-for-social-good

  Landscape analysis of AI4Good by McKinsey.

- **Accelerating Social Good with Artificial Intelligence: Insights from Google Impact Challenge**

  https://services.google.com/fh/files/misc/accelerating_social_good_with_artificial_intelligence_google_ai_impact_challenge.pdf

  An analysis of the over 2600 applications received from the Google Impact Challenge on the benefits, challenges, and opportunities. Also includes a useful taxonomy of project design, specific type of AI used, and data sets.

- **AI4Good Summit**

  https://aiforgood.itu.int/

  Annual conference that showcases research and prototypes in the AI4Good field.

- **X-Prize AI Impact Maps**

  https://impactmaps.xprize.org/

  Maps the current projects, opportunities, and challenges in specific problem areas.

- **Artificial Intimacy - Aspen Digital 2020 Report**

    https://csreports.aspeninstitute.org/Roundtable-on-Artificial-Intelligence/2020/report

ARTICLES AND BLOG POSTS

Chatbots and Nonprofits

- **Leveraging the Power of Bots for Civil Society: SSIR by Beth Kanter and Allison Fine**

    https://ssir.org/articles/entry/leveraging_the_power_of_bots_for_civil_society

    Provides an overview of opportunity and challenges of chatbots for civil society and a variety of use cases.

- **AI for Fundraising Today: Chatbots and Voice-Activated Fundraising by Beth Kanter**

    http://www.bethkanter.org/ai-link-roundup/

    Overview of chatbots and voice-activated technologies for fundraising campaigns.

- **AI for Fundraising: Special Report by the Chronicle**

    https://www.philanthropy.com/specialreport/a-i-and-fundraising-the-futu/201

    The potential of artificial intelligence to improve fundraising and the concerns that some in the charity world have about the new technology.

- **Nethope: Chatbots Made in Africa: Collective Lessons Learned**

    https://nethope.org/2021/05/26/chatbots-made-in-africa-collective-action-and-lessons-learned/

    Case studies on chatbots for international development work.

Machine Learning and Nonprofits

- **What Your Nonprofit Needs to Know About Machine Learning by GlobalGiving**

  https://www.globalgiving.org/learn/listicle/machine-learning-for-your-nonprofit

  A good primer on readiness.

- **Demystifying Machine Learning for Global Development by Sema Sgaier**

  https://ssir.org/articles/entry/demystifying_machine_learning_for_global_development#

  What nonprofits doing development work need to understand about AI4Good.

- **Artificial Intelligence: Snake Oil or Nonprofit Tool**

  https://radcampaign.com/blog/artificial-intelligence-snake-oil-or-powerful-nonprofit-tool?fbclid=IwAR04erm2F6JCrl-dVaT0HIV58VUIxe3hnJbJuQ7FjI7n7ENRfwv-niPTZUg

  Looks at the current use and potential of AI for online advocacy campaigns.

Human-Centered Design

- **Ideo.Org Design Kit: Methods**

  https://www.designkit.org/methods

  IDEO has been a thought leader in human-centered design methods. The design firm has a nonprofit spinoff (ideo.org) that focuses on methods for nonprofits and social change and includes many free practical resources and examples.

- **AI & Ethics: Collaborative Activities for Designers**

  https://www.ideo.com/post/ai-ethics-collaborative-activities-for-designers

  IDEO has also developed specific human-centered design methods for artificial intelligence, including these cards to help understand unintended consequences of smart technologies.

- **Luma System**

  https://www.luma-institute.com/about-luma/luma-system/

  The Luma system is one of the most practical, flexible, and versatile approaches to use for design thinking. It offers a playbook with simple techniques that anyone can use.

- **I Love Algorithms**

  https://dschool.stanford.edu/resources/i-love-algorithms

  Helps non-techies understand algorithms.

- **Mapping Problems to Solutions: Artificial Intelligence**

  https://dschool.stanford.edu/resources/map-the-problem-space

  Framework for thinking about mapping artificial intelligence to problems.

- **People + AI Guidebook**

  https://pair.withgoogle.com/

  The guidebook provides an overview of how human perception drives every facet of machine learning and offers up worksheets on how to get user input.

- **Designing Agentive Technology: AI That Works for People**

  By Christopher Noessel

  When designing chatbots and intelligent agents for automation, it should be grounded in human-centered design principles.

ABOUT THE AUTHORS

Photo credit: Trav Williams

Beth Kanter is an internationally recognized thought leader and trainer in digital transformation and well-being in the nonprofit workplace. She is the coauthor of the award-winning *Happy Healthy Nonprofit: Impact without Burnout* and coauthor with Allison Fine of the best-selling *The Networked Nonprofit*. Named one of the most influential women in technology by *Fast Company*, she has over three decades of experience in designing and delivering training programs for nonprofits and foundations. As a sought-after keynote speaker and workshop leader, she has presented at nonprofit conferences on every inhabited continent of the world to thousands of nonprofits. Learn more about Beth at www.bethkanter.org.

Photo credit: Margaret Fox Photography

Allison Fine is among the nation's preeminent writers and strategists on the use of technology for social good. She is the author of the award-winning *Momentum: Igniting Social Change in the Connected Age* and *Matterness: Fearless Leadership for a Social World* and coauthor with Beth Kanter of the best-selling *The Networked*

Nonprofit. She is a member of the national board of Women of Reform Judaism and was chair of the national board of NARAL Pro-Choice America Foundation and a founding board member of Civic Hall. She has keynoted conferences around the world. She and her husband, Scott Freiman, have three sons and live in Sleepy Hollow, New York. You can see more about Allison's work at www.allisonfine.com.

INDEX

209